T0113610

WHAT TO EXPECT *After* YOU REPENT WITH A SINCERE HEART

(Every Promise is received by Faith)

MAN'S PART GOD'S PART SATAN'S PART

ELDER BUFFIE SMITH

author**HOUSE**

AuthorHouse™
1663 Liberty Drive
Bloomington, IN 47403
www.authorhouse.com
Phone: 833-262-8899

Published by AuthorHouse   01/22/2022

ISBN: 978-1-6655-4874-8 (sc)
ISBN: 978-1-6655-4873-1 (hc)
ISBN: 978-1-6655-4879-3 (e)

Library of Congress Control Number: 2022900993

Print information available on the last page.

Contents

INTRODUCTION

Hello...My name is Elder Buffie Smith. Some people call me Buffie. Some people call me Elder Smith. And then some call me the name God gave me. Whichever name you decide to use will be alright with me. God renamed me back in 1999. I remember it like it was yesterday-because as the Prophet Jeremiah could say, "his word was in mine heart as a burning fire shut up in my bones!" (Refer to Jeremiah 20:9 KJV). Since then, I've made tons of mistakes, and because of them, I have experienced many setbacks. My disobedience caused me to get delayed so many times until I begin questioning if I was really called, or if I was really saved for that matter! I was so spiritually undeveloped and immature. If it had not been for Jesus making intercession on my behalf, God would have disqualified my behind countless times, but grace and mercy said wait!

Every time I think about where God has brought me from, I tell God how sorry I am all over again! And no, I don't say I'm sorry because I believe that God has not forgiven me, but because I can't believe how unfaithful I was to someone as sweet as Jesus; and yes, after all, he had done for me! But thanks be to God for his unconditional love towards sinners! Because thank to his love, not only am I still saved, but I am still called to serve at a provenance church in Dallas Texas where I've been a member for almost 20 years now. All I can say is thank you Lord for all you have done for me! But enough about me.

Anywho...I've written several books, but I believe the reason God had me write, "What to Expect AFTER you Repent" was so he could give teenagers, young adults, and anyone else who is serious about their salvation, another chance to get saved AND learn more about what takes place in the seen and unseen realm when MAN (male and female) get serious about our relationship with our Lord and precious Savior Jesus Christ.

As you read through my book, you will see scriptures from different versions of the bible. I believe God had me use different translations for

2 reasons. The first reason was so I could help make God's word easier to understand for those who struggle to understand the King James Bible. The second reason was so I could try to encourage those who accuse the bible of being boring, to read different versions. Because not only can this make study time intriguing, but what some will soon declare is worth doing. But again, a person can read the version of their choice. My goal is to lead sinners to Christ through whichever version works.

That said, I pray the scriptures underneath each topic will help those who are serious about their salvation to learn more about what GOD promises to do after a sinner repents, learn more about what SATAN will try to do after a sinner repents, and learn more about what MAN (male and female) must be willing to do after we repent with a sincere heart: because even though Ephesians 2:8 (in the NLT) says, God saved you by his grace when you believed. And you can't take credit for this; it is a gift from God. Salvation is not a reward for the good things we have done, so none of us can boast about it...can you believe that there are still some who have not received God's gift to sinners because they think God hates sinners?

Such news breaks my heart to pieces! Why? Because though it is a true saying that God hates sin, God does not hate sinners; else no human could be saved; seeing how ALL have SINNED and fall short of the glory of God (See Romans 3:23 NIV). And in another place, Romans 3:10 (ESV) says, "None is righteous, no, not one;"

Listen, I don't know who you are, or what led you to open my book-but what I do know is THAT IF YOU DECLARE WITH YOUR MOUTH THAT JESUS IS LORD AND BELIEVE IN YOUR HEART THAT GOD RAISED HIM FROM THE DEAD, YOU WILL BE SAVED according to Romans 10:9 in the NIV! It's just that simple little children! Romans 10:10 in the ESV says this, "FOR WITH THE HEART ONE BELIEVES AND IS JUSTIFIED, AND WITH THE MOUTH ONE CONFESSES AND IS SAVED!"

But before you get excited and put my book down, there's something I need to explain about Salvation that you probably haven't ever had explained to you before. Because you see, though getting saved from sin is simple, getting delivered from a sinful lifestyle is something that a Christian cannot achieve on their own! Such deliverance is something that only our Lord and sweet Savior can do AND is willing to do for all who declare that JESUS IS LORD! This is why it is so important for babes in Christ to sit under a Pastor where they can get fed the sincere milk of the word immediately and continuously after repenting with a sincere heart.

Not only can an anointed teacher of the word help (those who have not been set free from their sins) get free and stay free, but they can offer help in other ways too! It breaks my heart to see babes in Christ struggle with unclean spirits, lust, strongholds, and addictions months after declaring Jesus is Lord simply because they got saved from their sins, but they didn't get all the way delivered! And yes, I know getting hurt by other members in the body of Christ can cause (those who are not strong in the faith) to shy away from church but please don't let that become an excuse. All churches are not the same.

Many churches will embrace newcomers with open arms. But it's up to you and me to do our part in finding a Pastor that will give us a little of what we want and a lot of what we're going to need for us to experience every exceeding and precious promise that Christ died for us to have as we mature. This is another reason I believe God had me write, "What to expect AFTER we Repent!" Because not only will the scriptures underneath each topic show teenagers, young adults, and anyone else who is serious about their salvation more about what sinners can expect from God, but also, more about what God should be able to expect from each one of us.

Listen, we are living in the ending times! Bible prophesies are being fulfilled! And no, I'm not trying to put fear in teenagers and young adults, but I would hate for you, or myself to wake up early one morning and turn the news on, and hear how a group of people suddenly disappeared, and the people who saw them disappear told news reporters that they haven't ever witnessed such mystery, no, not in all history! Or even this; I don't want you or myself to turn on the news and hear how the traffic is backed up on your side of town because a group of people who were parked at a red light suddenly disappeared while waiting for the light to turn green!

So, if it's in your heart to get saved, do it now! Repent and be baptized while there is still time. (Because woe be to you and me if we miss (what many believe could be) the next big event on Heaven's Calendar! (Please read Revelation 19:9 and 1st Thessalonians chapter 4 and 5).

Again, I pray the scriptures underneath each topic will not only show teenagers, young adults, and anyone else who is serious about their Salvation, what God is willing to do for sinners but too, what we as sinners should be willing to do for God! Because who wants a one-sided relationship? Not me!

Now to help sinners remember what our part is, I'm asking every teenager, young adult, and anyone else who is serious about their eternal rewards to participate in the

#HEAVENLASTMINUTEREWARDCHALLENGE!

Because no matter how good it is to be saved, God still didn't send his only begotten son to die for the sins of the world just for sinners to get saved and not do something (each day) that will express gratitude in how we treat others. For example. We can express gratitude by being kind to our neighbors, family members, and friends. We can practice being kind to those we serve, and to those who serve us. We can practice being kind to those who don't deserve kind treatment and to those who do. We can donate food, clothes, our time, and money to charity. We can put our shopping cart back in its proper place. We can offer a homeless person food, clothes, or a warm blanket. We can give a neighbor a lift to work. We can clean up behind ourselves. We can offer help without expecting anything in return. We can mentor people without judging or telling their business. There are so many things we can do every day (whether big or small) to show God how much we appreciate our new King! Some call him Hosanna, others call him Emanuel! But the Bride of Christ calls him JESUS!

Please do not forget to participate in the #HEAVENLASTMINUTEREWARDCHALLENGE so we can receive a great warm welcome when we stand before the Son of Man on judgment day which could be real soon!

Revelation 22:12 (in the Amplified) says, "Behold, I (Jesus) am coming quickly, and My reward is with Me, to give each one according to the merit of his deeds (earthly works, faithfulness)." And Revelation 3:11 (NIV) says, "I am coming soon! Hold on to what you have so that no one will take your crown." And 2nd Corinthians 5:10 (Amplified) says, "For we (believers will be called to account and) must all appear before the judgment seat of Christ, so that each one may be repaid for what has been done in the body, whether good or bad (that is, each will be held responsible for his actions, purposes, goal, motives-the use or misuse of his time, opportunities and abilities)."

Until we meet again, love you, and thank you for supporting Jerusalem Ministries!

God's Part

Jeremiah 29:11 (NIV) "For I know the plans I have for you," declares the Lord, "plans to prosper you and not to harm you, plans to give you hope and a future."

Expect God to *FORGIVE* you

Forgive: To stop feeling angry or resentful toward (someone) for an offense, flaw or mistake. Excuse, overlook, disregard, pardon, exonerate. To cancel a debt.

1. **1ˢᵗ John 1:9 (KJV) If we confess our sins, he is faithful and just to FORGIVE us our sins, and to cleanse us from all unrighteousness.**

2. Psalm 103:10 (NIV) He does not treat us as our sins deserve...

3. **Micah 7:18 (GW) Who is a God like you? You FORGIVE sin and overlook the rebellion of your faithful people. You will not be angry forever, because you would rather show mercy.**

4. Romans 5:15 (NLT) But there is a great difference between Adam's sin and God's gracious gift. For the sin of this one man, Adam, brought death to many. But even greater is God's wonderful grace and his gift of FORGIVENESS to many through this other man, Jesus Christ.

5. **Psalm 65:3 (NLT) Though we are overwhelmed by our sins, you FORGIVE them all.**

6. Acts 10:43 (ESV) To Him all the prophets bear witness that everyone who believes in Him receives FORGIVENESS of sins through His name.

7. **Isaiah 43:25 (GNT) And yet, I am the God who FORGIVES your sins, and I do this because of who I am, I will not hold your sins against you.**

8. Psalm 103:12 (NLT) He has removed our sins as far from us as the east is from the west.

9. **Ephesians 1:7 (GW) Through the blood of his Son, we are set free from our sins. God FORGIVES our failures because of his overflowing kindness.**

10. Romans 4:5 (NLT) But people are counted as righteous, not because of their work, but because of their faith in God who FORGIVES sinners.

11. **Luke 6:37 (NIV) Do not judge, and you will not be judged. Do not condemn, and you will not be condemned. FORGIVE, and you will be FORGIVEN.**

12. Romans 8:1 (KJV) There is therefore now no condemnation to them which are in Christ Jesus, who walk not after the flesh, but after the Spirit.

13. **Colossians 1:14 (GW) His Son paid the price to free us, which means that our sins are FORGIVEN.**

14. Psalm 25:18 (KJV) Look upon mine affliction and my pain; and FORGIVE all my sins.

Expect God to *SAVE* you

Save: To keep someone or something safe; to preserve or guard from injury, destruction, or loss.

1. **John 10:28 (NIV) I give them eternal life, and they shall never perish; no one will snatch them out of my hand.**

2. John 3:16 (NIV) For God so loved the world that He gave his One and only Son, that whoever believes in him shall not perish but have eternal life.

3. **Lamentations 3:25-26 (GW) The Lord is good to those who wait for him, to anyone who seeks help from him. It is good to continue to hope and wait silently for the Lord to SAVE us.**

4. Romans 10:9 (Amplified) because if you acknowledge and confess with your mouth that Jesus is Lord (recognizing His power, authority, and majesty as God), and believe in your heart that God raised Him from the dead, you will be SAVED.

5. **Ephesians 2:8-9 (ESV) For by grace you have been SAVED through faith. And this is not your own doing; it is the gift of God, not a result of works, so that no one may boast.**

6. Titus 3:4-5 (NCV) But when the kindness and love of God our SAVIOR was shown, he SAVED us because of his mercy. It was not because of good deeds we did to be right with him. He SAVED us through the washing that made us new people through the Holy Spirit.

7. **Romans 8:30 (NIV) And those He predestined, He also called; those He called, He also justified; those He justified, He also glorified.**

8. John 3:36 (NIV) Whoever believes in the Son has eternal life, but whoever rejects the Son will not see life, for God's wrath remains on them.

9. **1ˢᵗ Corinthians 1:21 (Amplified) For since the world through all its (earthly) wisdom failed to recognize God, God in His wisdom was well-pleased through the foolishness of the message preached (regarding salvation) to SAVE those who believe (in Christ and welcome Him as Savior).**

10. John 3:17 (NIV) For God did not send his Son into the world to condemn the world, but to SAVE the world through him.

11. **Hebrews 7:25 (NLT) Therefore he is able, once and forever, to SAVE those who come to God through him. He lives forever to intercede with God on their behalf.**

12. Romans 10:13 (ESV) For everyone who calls on the name of the Lord will be SAVED.

Expect God to love you
UNCONDITIONALLY

Unconditionally: with no limits in any way: without restriction by conditions or qualifications; absolute

1. **John 15:13 (KJV) Greater love hath no man than this, that a man lay down his life for his friends.**

2. John 3:16 (NIV) For God so loved the world that he gave his one and only Son, that whoever believes in him shall not perish but have eternal life.

3. **Lamentation 3:22-23 (NIV) Because of the LORD'S great love we are not consumed, for His compassions never failed. They are new every morning; great is your faithfulness.**

4. Romans 8:37-39 (NIV) No, in all these things we are more than conquerors through Him who loved us. For I am convinced that neither death nor life, neither angels nor demons, neither the present nor the future, nor any powers, neither height nor depth, nor anything else in all creation, will be able to separate us from the love of God that is in Christ Jesus our Lord.

5. **1ˢᵗ John 4:16 (NIV) And so we know and rely on the love God has for us. God is love. Whoever lives in love lives in God, and God in them.**

6. Isaiah 54:10 (NIV) Though the mountains be shaken and the hills be removed, yet my unfailing love for you will not be shaken nor my covenant of peace be removed, says the Lord, who has compassion on you.

7. **Romans 5:8 (NIV) But God demonstrates his own love for us in this: While we were still sinners, Christ died for us.**

8. Galatians 2:20 (NIV) I have been crucified with Christ and I no longer live, but Christ lives in me. The life I now live in the body, I live by faith in the Son of God, who loved me and gave himself for me.

9. **Psalm 136:26 (NIV) Give thanks to the God of heaven. His love endures forever.**

10. Ephesians 2:4-5 (NIV) But because of his great love for us, God, who is rich in mercy, made us alive with Christ even when we were dead in transgressions-it is by grace you have been saved.

11. **Psalm 86:15 (CEV) But you, the Lord God, are kind and merciful. You don't easily get angry, and your love can always be trusted.**

12. Zephaniah 3:17 (NIV) The Lord your God is with you, the Mighty Warrior who saves. He will take great delight in you; in his LOVE he will no longer rebuke you, but will rejoice over you with singing.

13. **1st John 4:19 (KJV) We love Him, because He first loved us.**

14. 1st John 3:1 (GW) Consider this: The Father has given us his love. He loves us so much that we are actually called God's dear children. And that's what we are. For this reason the world doesn't recognize us, and it didn't recognize him either.

Expect God to have *MERCY* on you

Mercy: Compassion or forgiveness shown toward someone whom it is within one's power to punish or harm.

1. **Ephesians 2:4-5 (NLT) But God is so rich in MERCY, and He loved us so much, that even though we were dead because of our sins, He gave us life when He raised Christ from the dead. (It is only by God's grace that you have been saved!)**

2. Micah 7:18 (NIV) Who is a God like you, who pardons sin and forgives the transgression of the remnant of his inheritance? You do not stay angry forever but delight to show MERCY.

3. **Nehemiah 9:31 (NIV) But in your great MERCY you did not put an end to them or abandon them, for you are a gracious and MERCIFUL God.**

4. Hebrews 4:16 (NIV) Let us then approach God's throne of grace with confidence, so that we may receive MERCY and find grace to help us in our time of need.

5. **Psalm 51:1-2 (NIV) Have MERCY on me, O God, according to your unfailing love; according to your great compassion blot out my transgressions. Wash away all my iniquity and cleanse me from my sin.**

6. Proverbs 86:15 (CEV) But you, the Lord God, are kind and MERCIFUL. You don't easily get angry, and your love can always be trusted.

7. **Isaiah 55:7 (NIV) Let the wicked forsake their ways and the unrighteous their thoughts. Let them turn to the Lord, and he will have MERCY on them, and to our God, for he will freely pardon.**

8. Proverbs 28:13 (CEV) If you don't confess your sins, you will be a failure. But God will be MERCIFUL if you confess your sins and give them up.

Expect God to *CHANGE* you

Change: The act or instance of making or becoming different.

1. **Ephesians 4:22 (GW) You were taught to CHANGE the way you were living. The person you used to be will ruin you through desires that deceive you.**

2. 2nd Corinthians 5:17 (GW) Whoever is a believer in Christ is a new creation. The old way of living has disappeared. A new way of living has come into existence.

3. **Ephesians 4:23 (NCV) But you were taught to be made new in your hearts, to become a new person. That new person is made to be like God-made to be truly good and holy.**

4. Romans 12:2 (NLT) Don't copy the behavior and customs of this world, but let God transform you into a new person by CHANGING the way you think. Then you will learn to know God's will for you, which is good and pleasing and perfect.

5. **Colossians 3:9-10 (NCV) Do not lie to each other. You have left your old sinful life and the things you did before. You have begun to live the new life, in which you are being made new and are becoming like the One who made you. This new life brings you the true knowledge of God.**

6. 2nd Corinthians 4:16 (NCV) So we do not give up! Our physical body is becoming older and weaker, but our spirit inside us is made new every day.

7. **Philippians 4:8 (NCV) Brothers and sisters, think about the things that are good and worthy of praise. Think about the things that are true and honorable and right and pure and beautiful and respected.**

8. Romans 8:6 (NLT) So letting your sinful nature control your mind leads to death. But letting the Spirit control your mind leads to life and peace.

9. **2nd Corinthians 7:9 (NCV) Now I am happy, not because you were made sad, but because your sorrow made you CHANGE your lives. You became sad in the way God wanted you to, so you were not hurt by us in any way.**

10. Colossians 3:2 (NIV) Set your minds on things above, not on earthly things.

Expect God to give you *PEACE*

Peace: a stress-free state of security and calmness that comes when there is no fighting or war, everything coexisting in perfect harmony and freedom. It is a state of wholeness and completeness.

1. **Isaiah 26:3 (ESV) You keep him in perfect PEACE, whose mind is stayed on you, because he trusts in you.**

2. Romans 5:1 (NLT) Therefore, since we have been made right in God's sight by faith, we have PEACE with God because of what Jesus Christ our Lord has done for us.

3. **John 14:27 (NLT) I am leaving you with a gift-PEACE of mind and heart. And the PEACE I give is a gift the world cannot give. So don't be troubled or afraid.**

4. Numbers 6:26 (NLT) May the Lord show you his favor and give you his PEACE.

5. **Psalm 34:14 (NLT) Turn away from evil and do good. Search for PEACE, and work to maintain it.**

6. Proverbs 16:7 (ESV) When a man's ways please the Lord, He makes even his enemies to be at PEACE with him.

7. **2nd Thessalonians 3:16 (NIV) Now may the Lord of PEACE himself give you PEACE at all times and in every way...**

8. Psalm 29:11 (NIV) The Lord gives strength to His people; the Lord blesses His people with PEACE.

9. **Romans 15:13 (NIV) May the God of hope fill you with all joy and PEACE as you trust in him, so that you may overflow with hope by the power of the Holy Spirit.**

10. Colossians 3:15 (NLT) And let the PEACE that comes from Christ rule in your hearts. For as members of one body you are called to live in PEACE. And always be thankful.

Expect God to *USE* you

Use: The action of using something or the state of being used for a purpose; to utilize; make use of, take, hold, or deploy (something) as a means of accomplishing a purpose or achieving a result; employ.

1. **Philippians 1:6 (KJV) Being confident of this very thing, that he which hath begun a good work in you will perform it until the day of Jesus Christ.**

2. Ephesians 2:10 (ESV) For we are His workmanship, created in Christ Jesus for good works, which God prepared beforehand, so that we should walk in them.

3. **2ⁿᵈ Timothy 2:21 (NCV) All who makes themselves clean from evil will be USED for special purposes. They will be made holy, USEFUL to the Master, ready to do any good work.**

4. Mark 16:17-18 (KJV) And these signs shall follow them that believe; In my name shall they cast out devils; They shall speak with new tongues; They shall take up serpents; And if they drink any deadly thing, it shall not hurt them; They shall lay hands on the sick, and they shall recover.

5. **1ˢᵗ Corinthians 12:28 (NCV) In the church God has given a place first to apostles, second to prophets, and third to teachers. Then God has given a place to those who do miracles, those who have gifts of healing, those who can help others, those who are able to govern, and those who can speak in different languages.**

6. Philippians 2:13 (NLT) For God is working in you, giving you the desire and the power to do what pleases him.

7. **Hebrews 13:20-21 (ESV) Now may the God of peace who brought again from the dead our Lord Jesus, the great shepherd of the sheep, by the blood of the eternal covenant, equip you with everything good that you may DO His will, working in us that which is pleasing in His sight, through Jesus Christ, to whom be the glory forever and ever. Amen.**

8. 1ˢᵗ Corinthians 1:27-29 (CBS) Instead, God has chosen what is foolish in the world to shame the wise, and God has chosen what is weak in the world to shame the strong. God has chosen what is insignificant and despised in the world-what is viewed as nothing-to bring to nothing what is viewed as something, so that no one may boast in his presence.

Expect God to *CLEANSE* you

Cleanse: free someone from sin or quilt; (rid a person, place or thing) of something seen as unpleasant, unwanted, or defiling. Make something thoroughly clean; to wash.

1. **John 15: 3 (NIV) You are already CLEAN because of the word I have spoken to you.**

2. 1ˢᵗ John 1:9 (ESV) If we confess our sins, he is faithful and just to forgive us our sins and to CLEANSE us from ALL unrighteousness.

3. **Psalm 51:10 (ESV) Create in me a CLEAN heart, O God, and renew a right spirit within me.**

4. Ephesians 5:25-26 (ESV) Husbands, love your wives, as Christ loved the church and gave himself up for her, that he might sanctify her, having CLEANSED her by the washing of water with the word...

5. **1ˢᵗ John 1:7 (NLT) But if we are living in the light, as God is in the light, then we have fellowship with each other, and the blood of Jesus, his Son, CLEANSES us from all sin.**

6. Hebrews 9:13-14 (GW) The blood of goats and bulls and the ashes of cows sprinkled on unclean people made their bodies holy and CLEAN. The blood of Christ, who had no defect, does even more. Through the eternal Spirit he offered himself to God and CLEANSED our consciences from the useless things we had done. Now we can serve the living God.

7. **Hebrews 1:3 (NCV) The Son reflects the glory of God and shows exactly what God is like. He holds everything together with his powerful word. When the Son made people CLEAN from their sins, he sat down at the right side of God, the Great One in heaven.**

8. Titus 3:5 (NLT) He saved us, not because of the righteous things we had done, but because of his mercy. He washed away our sins, giving us a new birth and new life through the Holy Spirit.

9. **Ezekiel 36:25 (ESV) I will sprinkle CLEAN water on you, and you shall be CLEAN from all your uncleanness, and from all your idols I will CLEANSE you.**

Expect God to *DISCIPLINE* you when you purposely disobey his commandments

Discipline: To train (someone) to obey rules or a code of behavior, using punishment to correct disobedience.

1. **Psalm 103:10 (NIV) He does not treat us as our sins deserve...**

2. Job 5:17-18 (NIV) Blessed is the one whom God corrects; so do not despise the DISCIPLINE of the Almighty. For he wounds, but he also binds up; he injures, but his hands also heal.

3. **Revelation 3:19 (GW) I correct and DISCIPLINE everyone I love. Take this seriously, and change the way you think and act.**

4. Hebrews 12:7-9 (GW) Endure your DISCIPLINE. God corrects you as a father corrects his children. All children are DISCIPLINED by their fathers. If you aren't DISCIPLINED like the other children, you aren't part of the family. On earth we have fathers who DISCIPLINED us, and we respect them. Shouldn't we place ourselves under the authority of God, the father of spirits, so that we will live?

5. **Hebrews 12:10-11 (GW) For a short time our fathers DISCIPLINED us as they thought best. Yet, God DISCIPLINES us for our own good so that we can become holy like him. We don't enjoy being DISCIPLINED. It always seems to cause more pain than joy. But later on, those who learn from that DISCIPLINE have peace that comes from doing what is right.**

6. Proverbs 3:11-12 (NLT) My child, don't reject the Lord's DISCIPLINE, and don't be upset when he corrects you. For the Lord corrects those he loves, just as a father corrects a child in whom he delights.

7. **Proverbs 12:1 (NIV) Whoever loves DISCIPLINE loves knowledge, but whoever hates correction is stupid.**

8. Proverbs 10:17 (NLT) People who accept DISCIPLINE are on the pathway to life, but those who ignore correction will go astray.

9. **Psalm 94:12-14 (NIV) Blessed is the one you DISCIPLINE, Lord, the one you teach from your law; you grant them relief from days of trouble, till a pit is dug for the wicked. For the Lord will not reject his people; he will never forsake his inheritance.**

10. Deuteronomy 8:5-6 (NLT) Think about it: Just as a parent DISCIPLINES a child, the Lord your God DISCIPLINES you for your own good. So obey the commands of the Lord your God by walking in his ways and fearing him.

Expect God to help you *FINISH* your race

Finish: To bring (a task or activity) to an end; complete

1. **Jeremiah 29:11 (CEV) I will bless you with a future filled with hope-a future of success, not of suffering.**

2. Joshua 1:9 (NIV) Have I not commanded you? Be strong and courageous. Do not be afraid; do not be discouraged, for the Lord your God will be with you wherever you go.

3. **Isaiah 55:11 (NIV) So is my word that goes out from my mouth: it will not return to me empty but will accomplish what I desire and achieve the purpose for which I sent it.**

4. Jeremiah 32:27 (ESV) Behold, I am the Lord, the God of all flesh. Is anything too hard for me?

5. **Hebrews 10:35-36 (ESV) Therefore do not throw away your confidence, which has a great reward. For you have need of endurance, so that when you have done the will of God you may receive what is promised.**

6. Philippians 1:6 (ESV) And I am sure of this, that He who began a good work in you will bring it to completion at the day of Jesus Christ.

7. **Isaiah 40:31 (NLT) But those who trust in the Lord will find new strength. They will soar high on wings like eagles. They will run and not grow weary. They will walk and not faint.**

8. Matthew 24:13 (CEV) But if you keep on being faithful right to the end, you will be saved.

9. **1st Corinthians 9:24 (ESV) Do you not know that in a race all the runners run, but only one receives the prize? So run that you may obtain it.**

10. Galatians 6:9 (ESV) And let us not grow weary of doing good, for in due season we will reap, if we do not give up.

11. **Ecclesiastes 7:8 (ESV) Better is the end of a thing than its beginning, and the patient in spirit is better than the proud in spirit.**

12. 2nd Timothy 2:5 (ESV) An athlete is not crowned unless he competes according to the rules.

13. **Psalm 37:4 (ESV) Delight yourself in the Lord, and he will give you the desires of your heart.**

14. Colossians 3:23 (ESV) Whatever you do, work heartily, as for the Lord and not for men…

15. **Philippians 3:13-16 (NLT) No, dear brothers and sisters, I have not achieved it, but I focus on this one thing: Forgetting the past and looking forward to what lies ahead, I press on to reach the end of the race and receive the heavenly prize for which God, through Christ Jesus, is calling us…**

16. Ephesians 2:10 (ESV) For we are his workmanship, created in Christ Jesus for good works, which God prepared beforehand, that we should walk in them.

17. **Proverbs 20:24 (NKJV) A man's steps are of the Lord; How then can a man understand his own way?**

Expect God to let you be *BORN AGAIN*

Born-again: New, reborn, recreated, converted, changed, refreshed, reinvigorated, renewed, regenerated, redesigned, remodeled, reconstructed.

1. **John 3:7 (NIV) You should not be surprised at my saying, "You must be BORN AGAIN."**

2. Luke 11:13 (ESV) If you then, who are evil, know how to give good gifts to your children, how much more will the heavenly Father give the Holy Spirit to those who ask him!

3. **John 14:16 (CEV) Then I will ask the Father to send you the Holy Spirit who will help you and always be with you.**

4. 1ˢᵗ John 5:1 (ESV) Everyone who believes that Jesus is the Christ has been BORN of God, and everyone who loves the Father loves whoever has been BORN of him.

5. **1ˢᵗ Peter 1:3 (ESV) Blessed be the God and Father of our Lord Jesus Christ! According to his great mercy, he has caused us to be BORN AGAIN to a living hope through the resurrection of Jesus Christ from the dead...**

6. John 4:10 (NLT) Jesus replied, "If you only knew the gift God has for you and who you are speaking to, you would ask me, and I would give you living water."

7. **John 3:3 (ESV) Jesus answered him, "Truly, truly, I say to you, unless one is BORN AGAIN, he cannot see the kingdom of God."**

8. 1ˢᵗ Peter 1:23 (NCV) You have been BORN AGAIN, and this new life did not come from something that dies, but from something that cannot die. You were BORN AGAIN through God's living message that continues forever.

9. **1ˢᵗ John 3:9 (ESV) No one BORN of God makes a practice of sinning, for God's seed abides in him; and he cannot keep on sinning, because he has been BORN of God.**

10. Titus 3:5 (NLT) He saved us, not because of the righteous things we had done, but because of his mercy. He washed away our sins, giving us a new birth and new life through the Holy Spirit.

Expect God to *FILL* you with his Holy-Spirit

Fill: to make full; to occupy to the full capacity: to supply to an extreme degree or plentifully: Become an overwhelming presence in; pervade.

1. **John 7:38 (KJV) He that believeth on me, as the scripture hath said, out of his belly shall flow rivers of living water.**

2. Luke 1:67 (NIV) His father Zacharias was FILLED with the Holy Spirit and prophesied:

3. **Luke 4:1 (NIV) Jesus, full of the Holy Spirit, left the Jordan and was led by the Spirit into the wilderness...**

4. Acts 4:31 (NIV) After they prayed, the place where they were meeting was shaken. And they were all FILLED with the Holy Spirit and spoke the word of God boldly.

5. **Luke 1:15 (NASB) For he will be great in the sight of the lord; and he will drink no wine or liquor, and he will be FILLED with the Holy Spirit while still in his mother's womb.**

6. Acts 2:17 (NIV) In the last days, God says, I will pour out my spirit on all people. Your sons and daughters will prophesy, your young men will see visions, your old men will dream dreams.

7. **Ephesians 5:18-19 (NLT) Don't be drunk with wine, because that will ruin your life. Instead, be FILLED with the Holy Spirit, singing psalms and hymns and spiritual songs among yourselves, and making music to the Lord in your hearts.**

8. Acts 2:4 (NLT) And everyone present was FILLED with the Holy Spirit and began speaking in other languages, as the Holy Spirit gave them this ability.

9. **Romans 5:5 (ESV) And hope does not put us to shame, because God's love has been poured into our hearts through the Holy Spirit who has been given to us.**

10. Acts 7:55 (NIV) But Stephen, FULL of the Holy Spirit, looked up to heaven and saw the glory of God, and Jesus standing at the right hand of God.

11. **Romans 15:13 (NCV) I pray that the God who gives hope will FILL you with much joy and peace while you trust in Him. Then your hope will overflow by the power of the Holy Spirit.**

12. Acts 19:6 (NIV) When Paul placed his hands on them, the Holy Spirit came on them, and they spoke in tongues and prophesied.

Expect God to *WATCH* over you

Watch: observe and guard in a protective way. Follow closely or maintain an interest in. Look out or be on the alert for. An act or instance of carefully observing someone or something over a period of time.

1. **Genesis 28:15 (NIV) I am with you and will WATCH over you wherever you go, and I will bring you back to this land. I will not leave you until I have done what I have promised you.**

2. 1st Thessalonians 5:24 (Amplified) Faithful and absolutely trustworthy is He who is calling you (to Himself for your salvation), and He will do it (He will fulfill His call by making you holy, guarding you, WATCHING over you, and protecting you as His own).

3. **2nd Chronicles 16:9 (GW) The Lord's eyes scan the whole world to find those whose hearts are committed to him and to strengthen them…**

4. Psalm 32:8 (NIV) I will instruct you and teach you in the way you should go; I will counsel you with my loving eye on you.

5. **Proverbs 15:3 (GNT) The Lord sees what happens everywhere; He is WATCHING us, whether we do good or evil.**

6. Deuteronomy 32:10 (NIV) In a desert land He found him, in a barren and howling waste. He shielded him and cared for him; He guarded him as the apple of His eye…

7. **Psalm 121:8 (NIV) The lord will WATCH over your coming and going both now and forevermore.**

8. Jeremiah 1:12 (NIV) The Lord said to me, "You have seen correctly, for I am WATCHING to see that my word is fulfilled."

Expect God to give you *IRREVOCABLE* gifts

Irrevocable: Not able to be changed, reversed, or recovered; final.

1. **Romans 11:29 (NKJV) For the gifts and the calling of God are IRREVOCABLE.**

2. Luke 11:13 (ESV) If you then, who are evil, know how to give good gifts to your children, how much more will the heavenly Father give the Holy Spirit to those who ask him!

3. **James 1:17 (NIV) Every good and perfect gift is from above...**

4. 1ˢᵗ Peter 4:10-11 (NLT) God has given each of you a gift from his great variety of spiritual gifts. Use them well to serve one another. Do you have the gift of speaking? Then speak as though God himself were speaking through you. Do you have the gifts of helping others? Do it with all the strength and energy that God supplies. Then everything you do will bring glory to God through Jesus Christ. All glory and power to him forever and ever! Amen.

5. **1ˢᵗ Corinthians 7:7 (GW) I would like everyone to be like me. However, each person has a special GIFT from God, and these gifts vary from person to person.**

6. Romans 12:6-8 (NIV) We have different gifts, according to the grace given to each of us. If your gift is prophesying, then prophesy in accordance with your faith; if it is serving, then serve; if it is teaching, then teach; if it is to encourage, then give encouragement; if it is giving, then give generously; if it is to lead, do it diligently; if it is to show mercy, do it cheerfully.

7. **1st Corinthians 12:28 (ESV) And God has appointed in the church first apostles, second prophets, third teachers, then miracles, then gifts of healing, helping, administrating, and various kinds of tongues.**

8. 1st Corinthians 12:8-11 (NCV) The Spirit gives one person the ability to speak with wisdom, and the same Spirit gives another the ability to speak with knowledge. The same Spirit gives faith to one person. And, to another, that one Spirit gives gifts of healing. The Spirit gives to another person the power to do miracles, to another the ability to prophesy. And He gives to another the ability to know the difference between good and evil spirits. The Spirit gives one person the ability to speak in different kinds of languages and to another the ability to interpret those languages. One Spirit, the same Spirit, does all these things, and the Spirit decides what to give each person.

Expect God to *COMMUNICATE* with you

Communicate: to get someone to understand your thoughts or feelings. To convey knowledge of or information about: To make known. To transmit information, thought, or feeling so that it is satisfactorily received or understood. To reveal by clear signs.

1. **Luke 11:28 (ESV) But he said, "Blessed rather are those who HEAR the word of God and keep it."**

2. Romans 10:17 (NLT) So faith comes from HEARING, that is, HEARING the Good News about Christ.

3. **Hebrews 2:1 (ESV) Therefore we must pay much closer attention to what we have HEARD, lest we drift away from it.**

4. John 8:47 (NLT) Anyone who belongs to God listens gladly to the words of God. But you don't listen because you don't belong to God.

5. **Revelation 3:20 (NLT) Look! I stand at the door and knock. If you hear my voice and open the door, I will come in, and we will share a meal together as friends.**

6. Hebrews 3:15 (NLT) Remember what it says: "Today when you HEAR his voice, don't harden your hearts as Israel did when they rebelled."

7. **John 10:27 (ESV) My sheep HEAR my voice, and I know them, and they follow me.**

8. Deuteronomy 13:4 (ESV) You shall walk after the Lord your God and fear him and keep his commandments and obey his voice, and you shall serve him and hold fast to him.

9. **Exodus 19:19 (ESV) And as the sound of the trumpet grew louder and louder, Moses spoke, and God answered him in thunder.**

10. Galatians 3:5 (ESV) Does he who supplies the Spirit to you and works miracles among you do so by works of the law, or by HEARING with faith…

11. **Jeremiah 33:3 (ESV) Call to me and I will answer you, and will tell you great and hidden things that you have not known.**

12. 2nd Chronicles 7:15 (NIV) Now my eyes will be open and my ears attentive to the prayers offered in this place.

Expect God to *HEAL* you

Heal: to make well again.

1. **Psalm 30:2 (NIV) Lord my God, I called to you for help, and you HEALED me.**

2. Isaiah 53:5 (NLT) But he was pierced for our rebellion, crushed for our sins. He was beaten so we could be whole. He was whipped so we could be HEALED.

3. **Jeremiah 30:17 (NLT) "I will give you back your health and HEAL your wounds," says the Lord...**

4. James 5:16 (NIV) Therefore confess your sins to each other and pray for each other so that you may be HEALED. The prayer of a righteous person is powerful and effective.

5. **Exodus 23:25 (NIV) Worship the Lord your God, and his blessing will be on your food and water. I will take away sickness from among you...**

6. James 5:14-15 (NIV) Is anyone among you sick? Let them call the elders of the church to pray over them and anoint them with oil in the name of the Lord. And the prayer offered in faith will make the sick person well; the Lord will raise them up. If they have sinned, they will be forgiven.

7. **Deuteronomy 32:39 (NIV) See now that I myself am he! There is no god besides me. I put to death and I bring to life, I have wounded, and I will HEAL, and no one can deliver out of my hand.**

8. Psalm 41:3 (NCV) The Lord will give them strength when they are sick, and he will make them well again.

9. **Jeremiah 33:6 (NIV) Nevertheless, I will bring health and HEALING to it; I will HEAL my people and will let them enjoy abundant peace and security.**

10. 1st Peter 2:24 (NIV) He himself bore our sins, in his body on the cross, so that we might die to sins and live for righteousness; by his wounds you have been HEALED.

11. **Psalm 107:19-20 (NIV) Then they cried to the Lord in their trouble, and he saved them from their distress. He sent out his word and HEALED them; he rescued them from the grave.**

Expect God to *STRENGTHEN* you

Strengthen: to make stronger. The quality or state of being strong: capacity for exertion or endurance: power to resist force: power of resisting attack.

1. **Psalm 46:1 (KJV) God is our refuge and STRENGTH, a very present help in trouble.**

2. Isaiah 40:29 (NIV) He gives STRENGTH to the weary and increases the power of the weak.

3. **Isaiah 26:4 (KJV) Trust ye in the Lord for ever: for in the Lord Jehovah is everlasting STRENGTH.**

4. Isaiah 41:10 (NLT) Don't be afraid, for I am with you. Don't be discouraged, for I am your God. I will STRENGTHEN you and help you. I will hold you up with my victorious right hand.

5. **1ˢᵗ Chronicles 16:11 (NIV) Look to the Lord and his STRENGTH; seek his face always.**

6. Psalm 29:11 (NIV) The Lord gives STRENGTH to his people...

7. **Isaiah 40:31 (ESV) But they who wait for the Lord shall renew their STRENGTH; they shall mount up with wings like eagles; they shall run and not be weary; they shall walk and not faint.**

8. Philippians 4:13 (NKJV) I can do all things through Christ who STRENGTHENS me.

9. **Psalm 27:1 (NKJV) The Lord is my light and my salvation; Whom shall I fear? The Lord is the STRENGTH of my life; Of whom shall I be afraid?**

10. Psalm 18:1-2 (NCV) I love you, Lord. You are my STRENGTH. The Lord is my rock, my protection, my Savior. My God is my rock. I can run to him for safety. He is my shield and my saving STRENGTH, my defender.

11. **Psalm 22:19 (NIV) But you, Lord, do not be far from me. You are my STRENGTH; come quickly to help me.**

12. Psalm 73:26 (GNT) My mind and my body may grow weak, but God is my STRENGTH; he is all I ever need.

13. **2nd Thessalonians 3:3 (NIV) But the Lord is faithful, and he will STRENGTHEN you and protect you from the evil one.**

14. Psalm 28:7 (NIV) The Lord is my STRENGTH and my shield; my heart trusts in him, and he helps me. My heart leaps for joy, and with my song I praise him.

Expect God to *LEAD* and guide you

Lead: To cause (a person) to go with one by holding them by the hand. To show (someone) the way to a destination by going in front of or beside them. To be a route or means of access to a particular place or in a particular direction.

1. **John 8:12 (NLT) Jesus spoke to the people once more and said, "I am the light of the world. If you follow me, you won't have to walk in darkness, because you will have the light that LEADS to life."**

2. Galatians 5:16 (NLT) So I say, let the Holy Spirit guide your lives. Then you won't be doing what your sinful nature craves.

3. **Psalm 23:1-2 (NIRV) The Lord is my shepherd. He gives me everything I need. He lets me lie down in fields of green grass. He LEADS me beside quiet waters.**

4. Jeremiah 3:15 (NIV) Then I will give you shepherds after my own heart, who will LEAD you with knowledge and understanding.

5. **Psalm 25:9 (CEV) You LEAD humble people to do what is right and to stay on your path.**

6. Psalm 25:5 (NIV) Guide me in your truth and teach me, for you are God my Savior, and my hope is in you all day long.

7. **John 16:13 (NLT) When the Spirit of truth comes, he will guide you into all truth...**

8. Psalm 119:105 (NLT) Your word is a lamp to guide my feet and a light for my path.

9. **Proverbs 12:26 (NLT) The godly give good advice to their friends; the wicked LEAD them astray.**

10. Psalm 5:8 (NLT) LEAD me in the right path, O Lord, or my enemies will conquer me. Make your way plain for me to follow.

11. **Psalm 31:3 (NIV) Since you are my rock and my fortress, for the sake of your name LEAD and guide me.**

12. Isaiah 42:16 (NLT) I will LEAD blind Israel down a new path, guiding them along an unfamiliar way. I will brighten the darkness before them and smooth out the road ahead of them. Yes, I will indeed do these things; I will not forsake them.

13. **Psalm 119:133 (NLT) Guide my steps by your word, so I will not be overcome by evil.**

14. Proverbs 3:5-6 (NLT) Trust in the lord with all your heart; do not depend on your own understanding. Seek his will in all you do, and he will show you which path to take.

Expect God to give you
GODLY WISDOM

Godly Wisdom: is pure, peaceful, loving, gentle at all times, and willing to submit to others. It is full of mercy and the fruit of good deeds. It shows no favoritism and is always sincere: insight, good sense, good judgment; knowledge, and the capacity to make due use of it.

1. **James 1:5 (NIV) If any of you lacks WISDOM, you should ask God, who gives generously to all without finding fault, and it will be given to you.**

2. Proverbs 2:6 (NIV) For the Lord gives WISDOM; from his mouth come knowledge and understanding.

3. **Psalm 90:12 (NIV) Teach us to number our days, that we may gain a heart of WISDOM.**

4. Ephesians 1:17 (NIV) I keep asking that the God of our Lord Jesus Christ, the glorious Father, may give you the Spirit of WISDOM and revelation, so that you may know him better.

5. **Isaiah 55:8 (NIV) "For my thoughts are not your thoughts, neither are your ways my ways," declares the Lord.**

6. Proverbs 15:33 (CEV) Showing respect to the Lord will make you wise, and being humble will bring honor to you.

7. **Psalm 111:10 (ESV)** The fear of the lord is the beginning of WISDOM; all those who practice it have a good understanding...

8. Proverbs 13:20 (NLT) Walk with the wise and become wise; associate with fools and get in trouble.

9. **James 3:17 (NCV) But the WISDOM that comes from God is first of all pure, then peaceful, gentle, and easy to please. This WISDOM is always ready to help those who are troubled and to do good for others. It is always fair and honest.**

10. Colossians 4:5-6 (NCV) Be wise in the way you act with people who are not believers, making the most of every opportunity. When you talk, you should always be kind and pleasant so you will be able to answer everyone in the way you should.

11. **Psalm 19:7 (CEV) The Law of the Lord is perfect; it gives us new life. His teachings last forever, and they give WISDOM to ordinary people.**

12. Matthew 7:24 (NLT) Anyone who listens to my teaching and follows it is wise, like a person who builds a house on solid rock.

Expect God to help you avoid, escape and or endure *TEMPTATION*

Temptation: the desire to do something, especially something wrong or unwise. A situation in which one experiences a challenge to choose between fidelity and infidelity to one's obligations toward God.

1. **Matthew 6:13 (NCV) And do not cause us to be tempted, but save us from the Evil one...**

2. James 1:12 (NLT) God blesses those who patiently endure testing and TEMPTATION...

3. **Corinthians 10:13 (NLT) The TEMPTATIONS in your life are no different from what others experience. And God is faithful. He will not allow the TEMPTATION to be more than you can stand. When you are tempted, he will show you a way out so that you can endure.**

4. James 1:14-15 (NCV) But people are tempted when their own evil desire leads them away and traps them. This desire leads to sin, and then the sin grows and brings death.

5. **Matthew 4:10 (NLT) "Get out of here, Satan," Jesus told him. "For the Scriptures say, 'You must worship the Lord your God and serve only him.'"**

6. Romans 6:12 (NLT) Do not let sin control the way you live; do not give in to sinful desires.

7. **Galatians 5:16 (NLT) So I say, let the Holy Spirit guide your lives. Then you won't be doing what your sinful nature craves.**

8. Hebrews 2:18 (NIV) Because He himself suffered when He was tempted, He is able to help those who are being tempted.

9. **Romans 13:14 (GW) Instead, live like the Lord Jesus did, and forget about satisfying the desires of your corrupt nature.**

10. Romans 6:14 (CEV) Don't let sin keep ruling your lives. You are ruled by God's undeserved grace and not by the Law.

Expect God to be *FAITHFUL* to the end

Faithful: True to one's word, promises, vows, etc.

1. **1st Thessalonians 5:24 (Amplified) Faithful and absolutely trustworthy is He who is calling you (to Himself for your salvation), and He will do it (He will fulfill His call by making you holy, guarding you, watching over you, and protecting you as His own).**

2. 1st John 1:9 (NIV) If we confess our sins, he is FAITHFUL and just and will forgive us our sins and purify us from all unrighteousness.

3. **Psalm 145:17 (NIV) The Lord is righteous in all his ways and FAITHFUL in all he does.**

4. Deuteronomy 7:9 (NIV) Know therefore that the Lord your God is God; he is the FAITHFUL God, keeping his covenant of love to a thousand generations of those who love him and keep his commandments.

5. **2nd Thessalonians 3:3 (NIV) But the Lord is FAITHFUL, and he will strengthen you and protect you from the evil one.**

6. Lamentations 3:22-23 (NIV) Because of the Lord's great love we are not consumed, for his compassions never fail. They are new every morning; great is your FAITHFULNESS.

7. **Hebrews 10:23 (NCV) Let us hold firmly to the hope that we have confessed, because we can trust God to do what He promised.**

8. Isaiah 25:1 (GW) O LORD, you are my God. I will highly honor you; I will praise your name. You have done miraculous things. You have been completely reliable in carrying out your plans from long ago.

9. **Psalm 91:4 (GNT) He will cover you with his wings; you will be safe in his care; his FAITHFULNESS will protect and defend you.**

10. 1ˢᵗ Corinthians 1:9 (NIV) God is FAITHFUL, who has called you into fellowship with his Son, Jesus Christ our Lord.

11. **Psalm 143:1 (NIV) Lord, hear my prayer, listen to my cry for mercy; in your FAITHFULNESS and righteousness come to my relief.**

Satan's Part

Revelation 20:15 (NIV) Anyone whose name was not found written in the book of life was thrown into the lake of fire.

Expect Satan to tempt you to *SIN* in one or more of these areas so pray that "you enter not" into temptation daily!

Sin: to violate a moral or divine law of God. Deliberate disobedience to the known will of God.

1. **Matthew 7:1 (Amplified) Do not judge and criticize and condemn (others unfairly with an altitude of self-righteous superiority as though assuming the office of a judge), so that you will not be judged (unfairly).**

2. Proverbs 6:16-19 (NCV) There are six things the Lord hates. There are seven things he cannot stand: a proud look, a lying tongue, hands that kill innocent people, a mind that thinks up evil plans, feet that are quick to do evil, a witness who lies, and someone who starts arguments among families.

3. **Proverbs 11:13 (CEV) A gossip tells everything, but a true friend will keep a secret.**

4. James 2:1 (CEV) My friends, if you have faith in our glorious Lord Jesus Christ, you won't treat some people better than others.

5. **Exodus 20:13 (NIV) You shall not murder...**

6. 1st Corinthians 6:9-11(NIRV) Don't you know that evil people will not receive God's kingdom? Don't be fooled. Those who commit sexual sins will not receive the kingdom. Neither will those who worship statues of gods or commit adultery. Neither will men who are prostitutes or who commit homosexual acts. Neither will thieves or those who are often drunk or tell lies or cheat.

7. **Exodus 20:16 (NIV) You shall not give false testimony against your neighbor.**

8. 1ˢᵗ Peter 2:1 (CEV) Stop being hateful! Quit trying to *fool* people, and start being sincere. Don't be jealous or say cruel things about others.

9. **Matthew 15:11 (CEV) The food you put into your mouth doesn't make you unclean and unfit to worship God. The bad words that come out of your mouth are what make you unclean.**

10. Malachi 3:8 (NLT) Should people cheat God? Yet you have cheated me! But you ask, 'What do you mean? When did we ever cheat you?' You have cheated me of the tithes and offerings due to me.

11. **Hebrews 13:4 (GW) Marriage is honorable in every way, so husbands and wives should be faithful to each other. God will judge those who commit sexual sins, especially those who commit adultery.**

12. James 1:26 (NLT) If you claim to be religious but don't control your tongue, you are fooling yourself, and your religion is worthless.

13. **Exodus 20:12 (NIV) Honor your father and your mother, so that you may live long in the land the Lord your God is giving you.**

Expect to get *BLESSED* when persecuted for obeying Christ and doing what is right

Blessed: a favor or gift bestowed by God, thereby bringing happiness. The invoking of God's favor upon a person.

1. **Matthew 5:10 (NIV) BLESSED are those who are persecuted because of righteousness, for theirs is the kingdom of heaven.**

2. Romans 8:38 (NLT) And I am convinced that nothing can ever separate us from God's love. Neither death nor life, neither angels nor demons, neither our fears for today nor our worries about tomorrow-not even the powers of hell can separate us from God's love.

3. **Luke 6:22 (CEV) God will BLESS you when others hate you and won't have anything to do with you. God will BLESS you when people insult you and say cruel things about you, all because you are a follower of the Son of Man.**

4. Matthew 5:11-12 (NLT) God BLESSES you when people mock you and persecute you and lie about you and say all sorts of evil things against you because you are my followers. Be happy about it! Be very glad! For a great reward awaits you in heaven. And remember, the ancient prophets were persecuted in the same way.

5. **Isaiah 54:17 (NIRV) But no weapon that is used against you will succeed...**

6. 2nd Corinthians 12:10 (NIV) That is why, for Christ's sake, I delight in weaknesses, in insults, in hardships, in persecutions, in difficulties. For when I am weak, then I am strong.

7. **Mark 10:29-30 (GW) Jesus said, "I can guarantee this truth: Anyone who gave up his home, brothers, sisters, mother, father, children, or fields because of me and the Good News will certainly receive a hundred times as much here in this life. They will certainly receive homes, brothers, sisters, mothers, children and fields, along with persecutions. But in the world to come they will receive eternal life."**

8. John 16:33 (NCV) I told you these things so that you can have peace in me. In this world you will have trouble, but be brave! I have defeated the world.

9. **1st Peter 4:14 (NIRV) Suppose people make fun of you because you believe in Christ. Then you are BLESSED, because God's spirit rests on you. He is the Spirit of Glory.**

10. 1st Peter 3:14 (NLT) But even if you suffer for doing what is right, God will reward you for it. So don't worry or be afraid of their threats.

11. **Deuteronomy 28:7 (ESV) The Lord will cause your enemies who rise against you to be defeated before you. They shall come out against you one way and flee before you seven ways.**

12. Proverbs 16:7 (KJV) When a man's ways please the Lord, he maketh even his enemies to be at peace with him.

Expect your old sinful nature to *WAR* against your new divine nature

War: engagement in or the activities involved in war or conflict; competition, discord, fighting, rivalry, strife, struggle, contest, emulation, hostilities, strategy, striving, tug-of-war.

1. **Galatians 5:17 (NLT) The sinful nature wants to do evil, which is just the opposite of what the Spirit wants. And the Spirit gives us desires that are the opposite of what the sinful nature desires. These two forces are constantly fighting each other, so you are not free to carry out your good intentions.**

2. Romans 12:21 (NLT) Don't let evil conquer you, but conquer evil by doing good.

3. **1st Peter 2:11 (GW) Dear friends, since you are foreigners and temporary residents (in the world), I'm encouraging you to keep away from the desires of your corrupt nature. These desires constantly attack you.**

4. Romans 7:21 (GW) So I've discovered this truth: Evil is present with me even when I want to do what God's standards say is good.

5. **1st Corinthians 10:13 (NLT) The temptations in your life are no different from what others experience. And God is faithful. He will not allow the temptation to be more than you can stand. When you are tempted, He will show you a way out so that you can endure.**

6. James 4:7 (Amplified) So submit to (the authority of) God. Resist the devil (stand firm against him) and he will flee from you.

7. **1st Peter 5:8 (NCV) Control yourselves and be careful...**

Man's Part

Luke 18:1 (NLT) One day Jesus told his disciples a story to show that they should always pray and never give up.

Expect to express *SORROW*

Sorrow: Feeling or showing grief; sad, unhappy, regretful.

1. **2nd Corinthians 7:10 (NLT) For the kind of SORROW God wants us to experience leads us away from sin and results in salvation. There's no regret for that kind of SORROW. But worldly SORROW, which lacks repentance, results in spiritual death.**

2. James 4:9-10 (NLT) Let there be tears for what you have done. Let there be SORROW and deep grief. Let there be sadness instead of laughter, and gloom instead of joy. Humble yourselves before the Lord, and he will lift you up in honor.

3. **Psalm 51:17 (CEV) The way to please you is to feel SORROW deep in our hearts. This is the kind of sacrifice you won't refuse.**

4. 2nd Corinthians 7:9 (NCV) Now I am happy, not because you were made sad, but because your SORROW made you change your lives. You became sad in the way God wanted you to, so you were not hurt by us in any way.

5. **Psalm 34:18 (CEV) The Lord is there to rescue all who are discouraged and have given up hope.**

6. Isaiah 57:15 (NCV) And this is the reason: God lives forever and is holy. He is high and lifted up. He says, "I live in a high and holy place, but I also live with people who are sad and humble. I give new life to those who are humble and to those whose hearts are broken."

7. **Psalm 38:18 (NLT) But I confess my sins; I am deeply SORRY for what I have done.**

8. 2nd Chronicles 34:27 (NCV) When you heard my words against this place and its people, you became SORRY for what you had done, and you humbled yourself before me. You tore your clothes to show how upset you were, and you cried in my presence. This is why I have heard you, says the Lord.

9. **Psalm 147:3 (Amplified) He heals the brokenhearted and binds up their wounds (healing their pain and comforting their SORROW).**

10. 1st John 3:20 (CEV) But even if we don't feel at ease, God is greater than our feelings, and he knows everything.

11. **Ecclesiastes 7:3 (ESV) SORROW is better than laughter, for by sadness of face the heart is made glad.**

12. Joel 2:13 (NLT) Don't tear your clothing in your grief, but tear your hearts instead. Return to the LORD your God, for he is merciful and compassionate, slow to get angry and filled with unfailing love. He is eager to relent (show pity or mercy) and not punish.

13. **Psalm 6:6 (ESV) I am weary with my moaning; every night I flood my bed with tears; I drench my couch with my weeping.**

14. Matthew 5:4 (NASB) Blessed are those who mourn, for they will be comforted.

Expect to participate in a water *BAPTISM*

Water Baptism: a religious ceremony that involves a brief immersion in water, or water being sprinkled over the head or forehead as a symbol of washing away sin.

1. **Luke 3:21 (NIV) When all the people were being BAPTIZED, Jesus was BAPTIZED too...**

2. Acts 22:16 (NLT) What are you waiting for? Get up and be BAPTIZED. Have your sins washed away by calling on the name of the Lord.

3. **Matthew 28:19 (NIV) Therefore go and make disciples of all nations, BAPTIZING them in the name of the Father and of the Son and of the Holy Spirit...**

4. Mark 16:16 (NIV) Whoever believes and is BAPTIZED will be saved, but whoever does not believe will be condemned.

5. **Acts 10:48 (NIV) So he ordered that they be BAPTIZED in the name of Jesus Christ. Then they asked Peter to stay with them for a few days.**

6. 1ˢᵗ Peter 3:21 (NIV) And this water symbolizes BAPTISM that now saves you also-not the removal of dirt from the body but the pledge of a clear conscience toward God. It saves you by the resurrection of Jesus Christ…

7. **Acts 2:41 (NIV) Those who accepted his message were BAPTIZED, and about three thousand were added to their number that day.**

8. John 1:33 (NIV) And I myself did not know him, but the one who sent me to BAPTIZE with water told me, "The man on whom you see the Spirit come down and remain is the one who will BAPTIZE with the Holy Spirit."

9. **Mark 1:4 (NIV) And so John the Baptist appeared in the wilderness, preaching a BAPTISM of repentance for the forgiveness of sins.**

10. Romans 6:3-4 (NIV) Or don't you know that all of us who were BAPTIZED into Christ Jesus were BAPTIZED into his death? We were therefore buried with him through BAPTISM into death in order that, just as Christ was raised from the dead through the glory of the Father, we too may live a new life.

Expect to express *HUMILITY*

Humility: the quality or state of not thinking you are better than other people: the quality or state of being humble. A modest or low view of one's own importance; humbleness.

1. **Matthew 11:29-30 (NCV) Accept my teachings and learn from me, because I am gentle and HUMBLE in spirit, and you will find rest for your lives. The burden that I ask you to accept is easy; the load I give you to carry is light.**

2. Ephesians 4:2 (NLT) Always be HUMBLE and gentle. Be patient with each other, making allowance for each other's faults because of your love.

3. **Philippians 2:3 (NLT) Don't be selfish; don't try to impress others. Be HUMBLE, thinking of others as better than yourselves.**

4. Proverbs 11:2 (NCV) Pride leads only to shame; it is wise to be HUMBLE.

5. **Romans 12:16 (CEV) Be friendly with everyone. Don't be proud and feel that you are smarter than others. Make friends with ordinary people.**

6. James 4:10 (NLT) HUMBLE yourselves before the Lord, and he will lift you up in honor.

7. **1ˢᵗ Peter 3:3-4 (NCV) It is not fancy hair, gold jewelry, or fine clothes that should make you beautiful. No, your beauty should come from within you-the beauty of a gentle and quiet spirit that will never be destroyed and is very precious to God.**

8. Colossians 3:12 (GW) As holy people whom God has chosen and loved, be sympathetic, kind, HUMBLE, gentle, and patient.

9. **Proverbs 29:23 (Amplified) A man's pride and sense of self-importance will bring him down, but he who has a HUMBLE spirit will obtain honor.**

10. 1ˢᵗ Peter 5:6 (NLT) So HUMBLE yourselves under the mighty power of God, and at the right time he will lift you up in honor.

11. **Proverbs 22:4 (NLT) True HUMILITY and fear of the LORD lead to riches, honor, and long life.**

12. 2ⁿᵈ Chronicles 7:14 (GW) However, if my people, who are called by my name, will HUMBLE themselves, pray, search for me, and turn from their evil ways, then I will hear (their prayer) from heaven, forgive their sins, and heal their country.

13. **Isaiah 57:15 (NCV) And this is the reason: God lives forever and is holy. He is high and lifted up. He says, "I live in a high and holy place, but I also live with people who are sad and HUMBLE. I give new life to those who are HUMBLE and to those whose hearts are broken.**

Expect to *FORGIVE* God

Forgive: To stop feeling angry or resentful toward (someone) for an offense, flaw, or mistake; to wipe the slate clean, to pardon, to cancel a debt. Remission of an offense.

1. **Job 22:21 (GNT) Now, Job, make peace with God and stop treating him like an enemy; if you do, then he will bless you.**

Expect to *FORGIVE* yourself

Forgive: To stop feeling angry or resentful toward (yourself) for an offense, flaw, or mistake; to wipe the slate clean, to pardon, to cancel a debt. Remission of an offense.

1. **1ˢᵗ John 3:20 (NLT) Even if we feel guilty, God is greater than our feelings, and He knows everything.**

2. Romans 3:22-23 (NLT) We are made right with God by placing our faith in Jesus Christ. And this is true for everyone who believes, no matter who we are. For everyone has sinned; we all fall short of God's glorious standard.

3. **Philippians 3:13 (NLT) No, dear brothers and sisters, I have not achieved it, but I focus on this one thing: Forgetting the past and looking forward to what lies ahead...**

4. Proverbs 10:12 (NCV) Hatred stirs up trouble, but love FORGIVES all wrongs.

5. **Romans 8:1 (NKJV) There is therefore now no condemnation to those who are in Christ Jesus, who do not walk according to the flesh, but according to the Spirit.**

6. Proverbs 24:16 (ESV) For the righteous falls seven times and rises again...

Expect to *FORGIVE* others

Forgive: To stop feeling angry or resentful toward (someone) for an offense, flaw, or mistake; to wipe the slate clean, to pardon, to cancel a debt. Remission of an offense.

1. **Mark 11:25 (NIV) And when you stand praying, if you hold anything against anyone, FORGIVE them, so that your father in heaven may FORGIVE you your sins.**

2. Luke 6:37 (NIV) Do not judge, and you will not be judged. Do not condemn, and you will not be condemned. FORGIVE, and you will be FORGIVEN.

3. **1ˢᵗ Peter 3:9 (NIV) Do not repay evil with evil, or insult with insult. On the contrary, repay evil with blessing, because to this you were called so that you may inherit a blessing.**

4. Proverbs 10:12 (NCV) Hatred stirs up trouble, but love FORGIVES all wrongs.

5. **Proverbs 17:9 (NLT) Love prospers when a fault is FORGIVEN, but dwelling on it separates close friends.**

6. Galatians 6:1 (ESV) Brothers, if anyone is caught in any transgression, you who are spiritual should restore him in a spirit of gentleness. Keep watch on yourself, lest you too be tempted.

7. **Matthew 5:7 (ESV) Blessed are the merciful, for they shall receive mercy.**

8. Luke 17:3-4 (NIV) So watch yourselves. If your brother or sister sins against you, rebuke them; and if they repent, FORGIVE them. Even if they sin against you seven times in a day and seven times come back to you saying, 'I repent', you must FORGIVE them.

9. **1ˢᵗ Peter 4:8 (NCV) Most importantly, love each other deeply, because love will cause people to FORGIVE each other for many sins.**

10. Luke 6:27 (NLT) But to you who are willing to listen, I say, love your enemies! Do good to those who hate you.

11. **Colossians 3:13 (NLT) Make allowance for each other's faults, and FORGIVE anyone who offends you. Remember, the Lord forgave you, so you must FORGIVE others.**

Expect to keep God *FIRST*

First: To be more important than anyone or anything else; coming before all others.

1. **Matthew 6:33 (ESV) But seek FIRST the kingdom of God and his righteousness, and all these things will be added to you.**

2. Proverbs 3:6 (Living Bible) In everything you do, put God FIRST, and he will direct you and crown your efforts with success.

3. **John 15:5 (NLT) Yes, I am the vine; you are the branches. Those who remain in me, and I in them, will produce much fruit. For apart from me you can do nothing.**

4. Matthew 10:37-39 (NIV) Anyone who loves their father or mother more than me is not worthy of me; anyone who loves their son or daughter more than me is not worthy of me. Whoever does not take up their cross and follow me is not worthy of me. Whoever finds their life will lose it, and whoever loses their life for my name sake will find it.

5. **Exodus 20:3 (NIV) You shall have no other gods before me.**

6. Proverbs 3:9 (GW) Honor the Lord with your wealth and with the FIRST and best part of all your income.

7. **Matthew 22:37-38 (NIV) Jesus replied: "Love the Lord your God with all your heart and with all your soul and with all your mind.' This is the FIRST and greatest commandment."**

Expect to give thanks and be *THANKFUL*

Thankful: To show oneself grateful. Showing appreciation or gratitude.

1. **Colossians 4:2 (NIRV) Spend a lot of time in prayer. Always be watchful and THANKFUL.**

2. Ephesians 5:20 (NLT) And give THANKS for everything to God the Father in the name of our Lord Jesus Christ.

3. **Psalm 7:17 (NIV) I will give THANKS to the Lord because of his righteousness; I will sing the praises of the name of the Lord Most High.**

4. 1st Thessalonians 5:17-18 (NIV) Rejoice always, pray continually, give THANKS in all circumstances; for this is God's will for you in Christ Jesus.

5. **Hebrews 12:28-29 (NIV) Therefore, since we are receiving a kingdom that cannot be shaken, let us be THANKFUL, and so worship God acceptably with reverence and awe, for our God is a consuming fire.**

6. Philippians 4:6 (NLT) Don't worry about anything; instead, pray about everything. Tell God what you need, and THANK him for all he has done.

7. **Psalm 100:4 (NIV) Enter his gates with THANKSGIVING and his courts with praise; give THANKS to him and praise his name.**

8. Psalm 9:1 (NIV) I will give THANKS to you, LORD, with all my heart; I will tell of all your wonderful deeds.

9. **Colossians 2:6-7 (NIV) So then, just as you received Christ Jesus as Lord, continue to live your lives in him, rooted and built up in him, strengthened in the faith as you were taught, and overflowing with THANKFULNESS.**

10. Psalm 35:18 (CEV) And when your people meet, I will praise you and THANK you, Lord, in front of them all.

11. **Psalm 69:30 (NIV) I will praise God's name in song and glorify him with THANKSGIVING.**

12. Psalm 95:2 (ESV) Let us come into his presence with THANKSGIVING...

13. **Psalm 106:1 (NIV) Praise the Lord. Give THANKS to the Lord, for he is good; his love endures forever.**

14. Psalm 107:21-22 (NIV) Let them give THANKS to the Lord for his unfailing love and his wonderful deeds for mankind. Let them sacrifice THANK offerings and tell of his works with songs of joy.

Expect to *SERVE* God
with a good altitude

Serve: To perform duties or services for (another person or an organization); To be of used in achieving or satisfying; Function for or treat (someone) in a specified way.

1. **Hebrews 6:10 (NIV) God is not unjust; he will not forget your work and the love you have shown him as you have helped his people and continue to help them.**

2. Romans 12:11 (NCV) Do not be lazy but work hard, SERVING the Lord with all your heart.

3. **Deuteronomy 13:4 (NCV) SERVE only the Lord your God. Respect him, keep his commands, and obey him. SERVE him and be loyal to him.**

4. Luke 4:8 (NIV) Jesus answered, "It is written: Worship the Lord your God and SERVE Him only."

5. **Joshua 22:5 (NIV) But be very careful to keep the commandment and the law that Moses the servant of the Lord gave you: to love the Lord your God, to walk in obedience to him, to keep his commands, to hold fast to him and to SERVE him with all your heart and with all your soul.**

6. John 12:26 (NIV) Whoever SERVES me must follow me; and where I am, my servant also will be. My Father will honor the one who SERVES me.

7. **1ˢᵗ Samuel 12:24 (NIV) But be sure to fear the Lord and SERVE him faithfully with all your heart; consider what great things he has done for you.**

8. Luke 17:9-10 (NLT) And does the master thank the servant for doing what he was told to do? Of course not. In the same way, when you obey me you should say, "We are unworthy servants who have simply done our duty."

Expect to *SERVE* others as unto the Lord

Serve: To perform duties or services for (another person or an organization). To be of use in achieving or satisfying; Function for or treat (someone) in a specified way.

1. **Matthew 25:37-40 (NIV) Then the righteous will answer him, "Lord, when did we see you hungry and feed you, or thirsty and give you something to drink? When did we see you a stranger and invite you in, or needing clothes and clothe you? When did we see you sick or in prison and go to visit you?" The King will reply, "Truly I tell you, whatever you did for one of the least of these brothers and sisters of mine, you did for me."**

2. 1ˢᵗ Peter 4:10 (GW) Each of you as a good manager must use the gift that God has given you to SERVE others.

3. **Mark 10:45 (NIRV) Even the Son of Man did not come to be SERVED. Instead, he came to SERVE others...**

4. Matthew 23:11 (NIV) The greatest among you will be your servant.

5. **Hebrews 6:10 (NIV) God is not unjust; he will not forget your work and the love you have shown him as you have helped his people and continue to help them.**

6. Proverbs 19:17 (NIV) Whoever is kind to the poor lends to the Lord, and he will reward them for what they have done.

7. **Acts 20:35 (NIV) In everything I did, I showed you that by this kind of hard work we must help the weak, remembering the words the Lord Jesus himself said: 'It is more blessed to give than to receive.'**

8. Matthew 5:16 (NIV) In the same way, let your light shine before others, that they may see your good deeds and glorify your Father in heaven.

9. **Philippians 2:3-4 (NLT) Don't be selfish; don't try to impress others. Be humble, thinking of others as better than yourselves. Don't look out only for your own interests, but take an interest in others, too.**

10. Galatians 5:13 (NLT) For you have been called to live in freedom, my brothers and sisters. But don't use your freedom to satisfy your sinful nature. Instead, use your freedom to SERVE one another in love.

Expect to serve your ENEMIES as unto the Lord

Enemies: a person who feels hatred for, fosters harmful designs against, or engages in antagonistic activities against another; an adversary or opponent.

1. **Proverbs 25:21-22 (NCV) If your ENEMY is hungry, feed him. If he is thirsty, give him a drink. Doing this will be like pouring burning coals on his head, and the Lord will reward you.**

2. Luke 6:35 (NCV) But love your ENEMIES, do good to them, and lend to them without hoping to get anything back. Then you will have a great reward, and you will be children of the Most High God, because he is kind even to people who are ungrateful and full of sin.

3. **Matthew 7:12 (NCV) Do to others what you want them to do to you. This is the meaning of the law of Moses and the teaching of the prophets.**

4. Ephesians 6:7 (NIV) SERVE wholeheartedly, as if you were SERVING the Lord, not people...

5. **Matthew 5:44 (ESV) But I say to you, love your ENEMIES and pray for those who persecute you...**

6. Luke 6:28 (NIV) Bless those who curse you, pray for those who mistreat you.

Expect to *SEEK* God's presence and plan for your life daily

Seek: To search for (something); attempt to find (something). Attempt or desire to obtain or achieve (something).

1. **Matthew 6:33 (ESV) But SEEK first the kingdom of God and his righteousness, and all these things will be added to you.**

2. Psalm 63:1 (ESV) O God, you are my God; earnestly I SEEK you; my soul thirst for you; my flesh faints for you, as in a dry and weary land where there is no water.

3. **Hebrews 11:6 (ESV) And without faith it is impossible to please him, for whoever would draw near to God must believe that he exists and that he rewards those who SEEK him.**

4. Psalm 34:10 (ESV) The young lions suffer want and hunger; but those who SEEK the Lord lack no good thing.

5. **Luke 11:10 (ESV) For everyone who asks receives, and the one who SEEKS finds, and to the one who knocks it will be opened.**

6. Lamentations 3:25 (ESV) The Lord is good to those who wait for him, to the soul who SEEKS him.

7. **Psalm 119:2 (ESV) Blessed are those who keep his testimonies, who SEEK him with their whole heart...**

8. 2nd Chronicles 7:14 (ESV) If my people who are called by my name humble themselves and pray and SEEK my face and turn from their wicked ways, then I will hear from heaven and will forgive their sin and heal their land.

9. **Psalm 27:8 (ESV) You have said, "SEEK my face." My heart says to you, "Your face, Lord, do I SEEK."**

10. Isaiah 55:6 (ESV) SEEK the Lord while he may be found; call upon him while he is near.

11. **Psalm 34:4 (ESV) I sought the Lord, and he answered me and delivered me from all my fears.**

12. Colossians 3:1 (ESV) If then you have been raised with Christ, SEEK the things that are above, where Christ is, seated at the right hand of God.

13. **Proverbs 8:17 (ESV) I love those who love me, and those who SEEK me diligently find me.**

14. Psalm 14:2 (ESV) The Lord looks down from heaven on the children of man, to see if there are any who understand, who SEEK after God.

15. **Amos 5:4 (ESV) For thus says the Lord to the house of Israel; SEEK me and live;**

16. Psalm 9:10 (ESV) And those who know your name put their trust in you, for you, O Lord, have not forsaken those who SEEK you.

17. **1st Chronicles 16:10-11 (ESV) Glory in his holy name; let the hearts of those who SEEK the Lord rejoice! SEEK the Lord and his strength; SEEK his presence continually!**

Expect to *TESTIFY*

Testify: To make known; to make a statement based on personal knowledge or belief: bear witness; To make a solemn declaration under oath for the purpose of establishing a fact (as in court).

1. **Isaiah 12:4 (NCV) At that time you will say, "Praise the LORD and worship him. Tell everyone what he has done and how great he is."**

2. Acts 26:22-23 (NIV) But God has helped me to this very day; so I stand here and TESTIFY to small and great alike...

3. **Acts 5:42 (NIV) Day after day, in the temple courts and from house to house, they never stopped teaching and proclaiming the good news that Jesus is the Messiah.**

4. Matthew 5:13 (NCV) You are the salt of the earth. But if the salt loses its salty taste, it cannot be made salty again. It is good for nothing, except to be thrown out and walked on.

5. **Acts 20:24 (NIV) However, I consider my life worth nothing to me; my only aim is to finish the race and complete the task the Lord Jesus has given me-the task of TESTIFYING to the good news of God's grace.**

6. John 20:21 (NIV) Again Jesus said, "Peace be with you! As the Father has sent me, I am sending you."

7. **Acts 13:47 (NCV) This is what the Lord told us to do, saying: "I have made you a light for the nations; you will show people all over the world the way to be saved."**

8. Psalm 9:1 (NIV) I will give thanks to you, Lord, with all my heart; I will tell of all your wonderful deeds.

Expect to exercise your *FAITH*

Faith: complete trust or confidence in someone or something; Strong belief in God or in the doctrines of a religion, based on spiritual apprehension rather than proof.

1. **Hebrews 10:23 (GW) We must continue to hold firmly to our declaration of FAITH. The one who made the promise is FAITHFUL.**

2. Hebrews 12:1-2 (NCV) We are surrounded by a great cloud of people whose lives tell us what FAITH means. So let us run the race that is before us and never give up. We should remove from our lives anything that would get in the way and the sin that so easily holds us back. Let us look only to Jesus, the One who began our FAITH and who makes it perfect...

3. **Galatians 3:26 (KJV) For ye are all the children of God by FAITH in Christ Jesus.**

4. Luke 22:31-32 (NLT) Simon, Simon, Satan has asked to sift each of you like wheat. But I have pleaded in prayer for you, Simon, that your FAITH should not fail...

5. **Galatians 3:14 (NIV) He redeemed us in order that the blessing given to Abraham might come to the Gentiles through Jesus Christ, so that by FAITH we might receive the promise of the Spirit.**

6. Romans 3:30 (NLT) There is only one God, and he makes people right with himself only by FAITH, whether they are Jews or Gentiles.

7. **Galatians 2:20 (ESV) I have been crucified with Christ. It is no longer I who live, but Christ who lives in me. And the life**

I now live in the flesh I live by FAITH in the Son of God, who loved me and gave himself for me.**

8. Romans 12:3 (NLT) Because of the privilege and authority God has given me, I give each of you this warning: Don't think you are better than you really are. Be honest in your evaluation of yourselves, measuring yourselves by the FAITH God has given us.

9. **Ephesians 2:8-9 (ESV) For by grace you have been saved through FAITH. And this is not your own doing; it is the gift of God, not a result of works, so that no one may boast.**

10. 2nd Corinthians 5:7 (Amplified) For we walk by FAITH, not by sight (living our lives in a manner consistent with our confident belief in God's promises).

11. **Ephesians 3:16-17 (NIV) I pray that out of his glorious riches he may strengthen you with power through his Spirit in you inner being, so that Christ may dwell in your hearts through FAITH...**

12. 1st Corinthians 16:13 (NKJV) Watch, stand fast in the FAITH, be brave, be strong.

13. **Romans 1:17 (NIV) For in the gospel, the righteousness of God is revealed-a righteousness that is by FAITH from first to last, just as it is written: "The righteous will live by FAITH."**

14. Romans 14:23 (GW) But if a person has doubts and still eats, he is condemned because he didn't act in FAITH. Anything that is not done in FAITH is sin.

Expect to be *KIND* to everyone

Kind: having or showing a friendly, generous, and considerate nature.

1. **Romans 11:22 (NIRV) Think about how KIND God is! Also think about how firm he is! He was hard on those who stopped following him. But he is KIND to you. So you must continue to live in his KINDNESS. If you don't, you also will be cut off.**

2. Galatians 5:22-23 (NIV) But the fruit of the Spirit is love, joy peace, forbearance, KINDNESS, goodness, faithfulness, gentleness and self-control. Against such things there is no law.

3. **Ephesians 4:32 (NIV) Be KIND and compassionate to one another, forgiving each other, just as in Christ God forgave you.**

4. Proverbs 11:17 (NIV) Those who are KIND benefit themselves, but the cruel bring ruin on themselves.

5. **Colossians 3:12 (NIV) Therefore, as God's chosen people, holy and dearly loved, clothe yourselves with compassion, KINDNESS, humility, gentleness and patience.**

6. 1st Corinthians 13:4 (NIV) Love is patient, love is KIND...

7. **Proverbs 19:17 (NIV) Whoever is KIND to the poor lends to the Lord, and he will reward them for what they have done.**

8. Colossians 4:6 (NCV) When you talk, you should always be KIND and pleasant so you will be able to answer everyone in the way you should.

Expect to express *SELF-CONTROL*

Self-Control: restraint exercised over one's own impulses, emotions, or desires.

1. **Romans 6:12 (NLT) Do not let sin CONTROL the way you live; do not give in to sinful desires.**

2. Proverbs 19:11 (NLT) Sensible people CONTROL their temper; they earn respect by overlooking wrongs.

3. **Psalm 37:8 (NLT) Stop being angry! Turn from your rage! Do not lose your temper-it only leads to harm.**

4. Proverbs 25:28 (NIV) Like a city whose walls are broken through is a person who lacks SELF-CONTROL.

5. **Romans 6:16 (NLT) Don't you realize that you become the slave of whatever you choose to obey? You can be a slave to sin, which leads to death, or you can choose to obey God, which leads to righteous living.**

6. 2nd Peter 1:5-7 (NCV) Because you have these blessing, do your best to add these things to your lives: to your faith, add goodness; and to your goodness, add knowledge; and to your knowledge, add SELF-CONTROL; and to your SELF-CONTROL, add patience; and to your patience, add service for God; and to your service for God, add kindness for your brothers and sisters in Christ; and to this kindness, add love.

7. **Proverbs 16:32 (NCV) Patience is better than strength. Controlling your temper is better than capturing a city.**

8. Romans 8:5 (NLT) Those who are dominated by the sinful nature think about sinful things, but those who are CONTROLLED by the Holy Spirit think about things that please the Spirit.

9. **2nd Timothy 1:7 (NCV) God did not give us a spirit that makes us afraid but a spirit of power and love and SELF-CONTROL**

10. Job 31:1 (NIV) I made a covenant with my eyes not to look lustfully at a young woman.

Expect to express *PATIENCE*

Patience: the capacity to accept or tolerate delay, trouble, or suffering without getting angry or upset.

1. **Proverbs 15:18 (NLT) A hot-tempered person starts fights; a cool-tempered person stops them.**

2. 1st Corinthians 13:4 (NASB95) Love is PATIENT, love is kind and is not jealous; love does not brag and it is not arrogant...

3. **Proverbs 14:29 (CEB) PATIENCE leads to abundant understanding, but impatience leads to stupid mistakes.**

4. Romans 8:25 (ESV) But if we hope for what we do not see, we wait for it with PATIENCE.

5. **Exodus 14:14 (CEB) The Lord will fight for you. You just keep still.**

6. Galatians 5:22 (ESV) But the fruit of the Spirit is love, joy, peace, PATIENCE...

7. **Proverbs 16:32 (NCV) PATIENCE is better than strength. Controlling your temper is better than capturing a city.**

8. 2nd Timothy 4:2 (CEB) Preach the word. Be ready to do it whether it is convenient or inconvenient. Correct, confront, and encourage with PATIENCE and instruction.

9. **Galatians 6:9 (NLT) So let's not get tired of doing what is good. At just the right time we will reap a harvest of blessing if we don't give up.**

10. Ephesians 4:2 (NCV) Always be humble, gentle, and PATIENT, accepting each other in love.

11. **Lamentations 3:26 (NIRV) It is good when people WAIT quietly for the Lord to save them.**

12. Ecclesiastes 7:8 (NLT) Finishing is better than starting. PATIENCE is better than pride.

13. **James 5:8 (NCV) You, too, must be PATIENT. Do not give up hope, because the Lord is coming soon.**

14. Colossians 3:12 (CEB) Therefore, as God's choice, holy and loved, put on compassion, kindness, humility, gentleness, and PATIENCE.

Expect to read and *STUDY* God's word

Study: to read with detail especially with the intention of learning; meditate; sustained purposeful concentration and attention to details and minutiae.

1. **Matthew 4:4 (NLT) But Jesus told him, "No! The scripture say, People do not live by bread alone, but by every word that comes from the mouth of God."**

2. Matthew 11:29 (NCV) Accept my teachings and learn from me, because I am gentle and humble in spirit, and you will find rest for your lives.

3. **Psalm 34:8 (NCV) Examine and see how good the Lord is. Happy is the person who trusts him.**

4. Colossians 3:16 (NIV) Let the message of Christ dwell among you richly as you teach and admonish one another with all wisdom through psalms, hymns, and songs from the Spirit, singing to God with gratitude in your hearts.

5. **Romans 12:2 (NLT) Don't copy the behavior and customs of this world, but let God transform you into a new person by changing the way you think. Then you will learn to know God's will for you, which is good and pleasing and perfect.**

6. Psalm 119:11 (NLT) I have hidden your word in my heart, that I might not sin against you.

7. **2nd Timothy 2:15 (NCV) Make every effort to give yourself to God as the kind of person he will approve. Be a worker who is not ashamed and who uses the true teaching in the right way.**

8. Ephesians 6:17 (CEV) Let God's saving power be like a helmet, and for a sword use God's message that comes from the Spirit.

9. **James 1:25 (NCV) But the truly happy people are those who carefully STUDY God's perfect law that makes people free, and they continue to STUDY it. They do not forget what they heard, but they obey what God's teaching says. Those who do this will be made happy.**

10. Psalm 1:1-2 (NIRV) Blessed is the person who obeys the law of the Lord. They don't follow the advice of evil people. They don't make a habit of doing what sinners do. They don't join those who make fun of the Lord and his law. Instead, the law of the Lord gives them joy. They think about his law day and night.

Expect to *PROSPER* after you have done the work

Prosper: to cause to succeed or thrive: to become strong and flourishing.

1. **Jeremiah 29:11 (NIV) "For I know the plans I have for you," declares the Lord, "plans to PROSPER you and not to harm you, plans to give you hope and a future."**

2. Deuteronomy 29:9 (NIV) Carefully follow the terms of this covenant, so that you may PROSPER in everything you do.

3. **Proverbs 13:4 (NLT) Lazy people want much but get little, but those who work hard will PROSPER.**

4. Psalm 75:6-7 (KJV) For promotion cometh neither from the east, nor from the west, nor from the south. But God is the judge; he putteth down one, and setteth up another.

5. **3rd John 1:2 (NKJV) Beloved, I pray that you may PROSPER in all things and be in health, just as your soul PROSPERS.**

6. Psalm 1:1-3 (NIRV) Blessed is the person who obeys the law of the Lord. They don't follow the advice of evil people. They don't make a habit of doing what sinners do. They don't join those who make fun of the Lord and his law. Instead, the law of the Lord gives them joy. They think about his law day and night. That kind of person is like a tree that is planted near a stream of water. It always bears its fruit at the right time. Its leaves don't dry up. Everything godly people do turns out well.

7. **Psalm 23:1 (NLT) The Lord is my shepherd, I have all that I need.**

8. Joshua 1:8 (ESV) This Book of the Law shall not depart from your mouth, but you shall meditate on it day and night, so that you may be careful to do according to all that is written in it. For then you will make your way PROSPEROUS, and then you will have good success.

9. **Job 36:11 (Amplified) If they hear and serve Him, they will end their days in PROSPERITY and their years in pleasantness and joy.**

10. Deuteronomy 30:8-9 (NLT) Then you will again obey the Lord and keep all his commands that I am giving you today. The Lord your God will then make you successful in everything you do...

11. **Proverbs 28:25 (GW) A greedy person stirs up a fight, but whoever trusts the Lord PROSPERS.**

12. Genesis 39:2 (ESV) The Lord was with Joseph, and he became a successful man...

13. **Proverbs 11:25 (NIV) A generous person will PROSPER; whoever refreshes others will be refreshed.**

14. Psalm 115:14 (NIV) May the Lord cause you to flourish, both you and your children.

15. **Job 8:7 (NLT) And though you started with little, you will end with much.**

Expect to love God
UNCONDITIONALLY

Unconditionally: with no limits in any way: without restriction by conditions or qualifications; ABSOLUTE.

1. **John 14:21 (NIV) Whoever has my commands and keeps them is the one who loves me. The one who loves me will be loved by my Father, and I too will love them and show myself to them.**

2. Hebrews 6:10 (NIV) God is not unjust; He will not forget your work and the love you have shown Him as you have helped His people and continue to help them.

3. **Proverbs 21:3 (ERV) Do what is right and fair. The Lord loves that more than sacrifices.**

4. Joshua 22:5 (NIV) But be very careful to keep the commandment and the law that Moses the servant of the Lord gave you: to love the Lord your God, to walk in obedience to Him, to keep His commands, to hold fast to Him and to serve Him with all your heart and with all your soul.

5. **Romans 8:28 (NLT) And we know that God causes everything to work together for the good of those who love God and are called according to His purpose for them.**

6. Matthew 22:37-38 (NIV) Jesus replied: "Love the Lord your God with all your heart and with all your soul and with all your mind. This is the first and greatest commandment."

7. **1ˢᵗ John 3:17 (NIV) If anyone has material possessions and sees a brother or sister in need but has no pity on them, how can the love of God be in that person?**

8. James 2:5 (NIV) Listen, my dear brothers and sisters: "Has not God chosen those who are poor in the eyes of the world to be rich in faith and to inherit the kingdom he promised those who love him?"

9. **1ˢᵗ John 4:8 (NIV) Whoever does not love does not know God, because God is love.**

10. Deuteronomy 7:9 (NIV) Know therefore that the Lord your God is God; He is the faithful God, keeping his covenant of love to a thousand generations of those who Love Him and keep his commandments.

11. **Psalm 116:1-2 (NIV) I love the LORD, for He heard my voice; He heard my cry for mercy. Because He turned his ear to me, I will call on him as long as I live.**

12. Psalm 31:23 (NIV) Love the Lord, all his faithful people! The Lord preserves those who are true to Him, but the proud He pays back in full.

13. **1ˢᵗ John 5:3 (NIV) In fact, this is love for God: to keep His commands. And His commands are not burdensome...**

14. Joshua 23:11 (NIV) So be very careful to love the Lord your God.

Expect to *LOVE* others unconditionally

Love: is patient, love is kind. It does not envy, it does not boast, it is not proud. It does not dishonor others, it is not self-seeking, it is not easily angered, it keeps no record of wrongs. Wanting good to come to another person; being concerned and willing to work for another person's benefit.

1. **John 15:12 (ESV) This is my commandment, that you LOVE one another as I have LOVED you.**

2. Romans 13:8 (NLT) Owe nothing to anyone-except for your obligation to LOVE one another. If you LOVE your neighbor, you will fulfill the requirements of God's law.

3. **1st Thessalonians 3:12 (NIV) May the Lord make your LOVE increase and overflow for each other and for everyone else, just as ours does for you.**

4. 1st John 4:8 (NIV) Whoever does not LOVE does not know God, because God is LOVE.

5. **Proverbs 10:12 (NIV) Hatred stirs up conflict, but LOVE covers over all wrongs.**

6. 1st John 4:12 (NIV) No one has ever seen God; but if we LOVE one another, God lives in us and his LOVE is made complete in us.

7. **Romans 12:10 (NCV) LOVE each other like brothers and sisters. Give each other more honor than you want for yourselves.**

8. 1ˢᵗ Corinthians 16:14 (NIV) Do everything in LOVE.

9. **Colossians 3:14 (NCV) Even more than all this, clothe yourself in LOVE. LOVE is what holds you all together in perfect unity.**

10. Proverbs 3:3-4 (NIV) Let LOVE and faithfulness never leave you; bind them around your neck, write them on the tablet of your heart. Then you will win favor and a good name in the sight of God and man.

11. **Ephesians 4:2 (NLT) Always be humble and gentle. Be patient with each other, making allowance for each other's faults because of your LOVE.**

12. 1ˢᵗ Peter 4:8 (NCV) Most importantly, LOVE each other deeply, because LOVE will cause people to forgive each other for many sins.

13. **Romans 12:9-10 (NLT) Don't just pretend to LOVE others. Really LOVE them. Hate what is wrong. Hold tightly to what is good. LOVE each other with genuine affection, and take delight in honoring each other.**

14. Hebrews 13:1-2 (NIV) Keep on LOVING one another as brothers and sisters. Do not forget to show hospitality to strangers, for by so doing some people have shown hospitality to angels without knowing it.

Expect to *PRAY* about everything

Pray: is how believers of God talk to him. It is how they make their praise and requests known. It is a way of relating to God. To hope strongly for a particular outcome.

1. Philippians 4:6 (NLT) Don't worry about anything; instead, PRAY about everything. Tell God what you need, and thank him for all he has done.

2. **1st Thessalonians 5:17 (NCV) PRAY continually...**

3. Matthew 6:6 (NLT) But when you PRAY, go away by yourself, shut the door behind you, and PRAY to your Father in private. Then your Father, who sees everything, will reward you.

4. **Matthew 6:7-8 (NCV) And when you PRAY, don't be like those people who don't know God. They continue saying things that mean nothing, thinking that God will hear them because of their many words. Don't be like them, because your Father knows the things you need before you ask him.**

5. Colossians 4:2 (NIV) Devote yourselves to PRAYER, being watchful and thankful.

6. **Psalm 145:18 (NIV) The LORD is near to all who call on him, to all who call on him in truth.**

7. Matthew 26:41 (NIV) Watch and PRAY so that you will not fall into temptation. The spirit is willing, but the flesh is weak.

8. **Job 22:27 (NIV) You will PRAY to him, and he will hear you, and you will fulfill your vows.**

9. James 5:13 (NIV) Is anyone among you in trouble? Let them PRAY...

10. **Mark 11:24 (NIV) Therefore, I tell you, whatever you ask for in PRAYER, believe that you have received it, and it will be yours.**

11. Psalm 102:17 (NCV) He will answer the PRAYERS of the needy; he will not reject their PRAYERS.

12. **Romans 12:12 (NCV) Be joyful because you have hope. Be patient when trouble comes, and PRAY at all times.**

13. Psalm 4:1 (NCV) Answer me when I PRAY to you, my God who does what is right. Make things easier for me when I am in trouble. Have mercy on me and hear my PRAYER.

14. **Proverbs 15:29 (NIV) The LORD is far from the wicked, but he hears the PRAYER of the righteous.**

15. Luke 18:1 (NIV) Then Jesus told his disciples a parable to show them that they should always PRAY and not give up.

16. **James 5:16 (NIV) Therefore confess your sins to each other and PRAY for each other so that you may be healed. The PRAYER of a righteous person is powerful and effective.**

Expect to *OBEY* God in good and bad times

Obey: comply with the command, direction, or request of (a person or a law); carry out (a command or instruction); to hear, trust, submit and surrender to God and his word.

1. **2ⁿᵈ Chronicles 30:8 (CEV) Don't be stubborn like your ancestors. Decide now to OBEY the Lord our God...**

2. Psalm 128:1 (CEV) The Lord will bless you if you respect him and OBEY his laws.

3. **James 1:22 (NLT) But don't just listen to God's word. You must do what it says...**

4. 1ˢᵗ Samuel 15:22 (CEV) "Tell me," Samuel said. "Does the Lord really want sacrifices and offerings? No! He doesn't want your sacrifices. He wants you to OBEY him."

5. **Leviticus 19:32 (CEV) I command you to show respect for older people and to OBEY Me with fear and trembling.**

6. Matthew 26:39 (NCV) After walking a little farther away from them, Jesus fell to the ground and prayed, "My Father, if it is possible, do not give me this cup of suffering. BUT DO WHAT YOU WANT, NOT WHAT I WANT."

7. **Hebrews 5:8 (NLT) Even though Jesus was God's Son, he learned OBEDIENCE from the things he suffered.**

8. Job 22:21 (NCV) OBEY God and be at peace with him; this is the way to happiness.

Expect to obey and honor your *PARENTS*

Parents: a father or mother.

1. **Ephesian 6:1 (NASB) Children, obey your parents in the Lord, for this is right.**

2. Proverbs 6:20 (Amplified) My son, be guided by your father's (God-given) commandment (instruction) and do not reject the teaching of your mother;

3. **Ephesians 6:2-3 (NIV) HONOR your father and mother-which is the first commandment with a promise-so that it may go well with you and that you may enjoy long life on the earth.**

4. Deuteronomy 5:16 (ISV) HONOR your father and your mother, just as the LORD your God commanded you...

5. **Exodus 20:12 (NIV) HONOR your father and your mother...**

6. Deuteronomy 27:16 (NIV) Cursed is anyone who dishonors their father or mother...

7. **Proverbs 19:26 (NLT) Children who mistreat their father or chase away their mother are an embarrassment and a public disgrace.**

8. Proverbs 20:20 (NLT) If you insult your father or mother, your light will be snuffed out in total darkness.

Expect to obey and honor your *PASTOR*

Pastor: a minister in charge of a Christian church or congregation.

1. **Hebrews 13:17 (NLT) Obey your spiritual leaders, and do what they say. Their work is to watch over your souls, and they are accountable to God. Give them reason to do this with joy and not with sorrow. That would certainly not be for your benefit.**

2. Acts 20:28 (NIV) Keep watch over yourselves and all the flock of which the Holy Spirit has made you overseers. Be shepherds of the church of God, which he bought with his own blood.

3. **Jeremiah 3:15 (NIV) Then I will give you shepherds after my own heart, who will lead you with knowledge and understanding.**

Expect to obey *AUTHORITY*

Authority: a person who has authority over another person. A person whose real or apparent authority over others inspires or demands obedience and emulation.

1. **1st Peter 2:13-14 (NLT) For the Lord's sake, submit to all human AUTHORITY-whether the king as head of state, or the officials he has appointed. For the king has sent them to punish those who do wrong and to honor those who do right.**

2. Titus 3:1 (NLT) Remind the believers to submit to the government and its officers. They should be obedient, always ready to do what is good.

3. **Romans 13:3 (NLT) For the AUTHORITIES do not strike fear in people who are doing right, but those who are doing wrong. Would you like to live without fear of the AUTHORITIES? Do what is right, and they will honor you.**

4. Romans 13:7 (NLT) Give to everyone what you owe them: Pay your taxes and government fees to those who collect them, and give respect and honor to those who are in AUTHORITY.

5. **Mark 12:17 (NLT) "Well, then," Jesus said, "Give to Caesar what belongs to Caesar, and give to God what belongs to God..."**

6. 1st Timothy 2:2-3 (NLT) Pray this way for kings and all who are in AUTHORITY so that we can live peaceful and quiet lives marked by godliness and dignity. This is good and pleases God our Savior...

Expect to obey and honor your *SPOUSE*

Spouse: A married person (husband or wife); better half, consort, mate, partner, significant other.

1. **Philippians 2:5 (NIV) In your relationships with one another, have the same mindset as Christ Jesus:**

2. Proverbs 18:22 (NLT) The man who finds a wife finds a treasure, and he receives favor from the LORD.

3. **1st Peter 3:1-2 (NIV) Wives, in the same way submit yourselves to your own husbands so that, if any of them do not believe the word, they may be won over without words by the behavior of their wives, when they see the purity and reverence of your lives.**

4. Colossians 3:19 (NIV) Husbands, love your wives and do not be harsh with them.

5. **1st Peter 3:5 (NIV) For this is the way the holy women of the past who put their hope in God used to adorn themselves. They submitted themselves to their own husbands...**

6. 1st Peter 3:7 (NIV) Husbands, in the same way be considerate as you live with your wives, and treat them with respect as the weaker partner and as heirs with you of the gracious gift of life, so that nothing will hinder your prayers.

7. **Colossians 3:18 (NIV) Wives, submit yourselves to your husbands, as is fitting in the Lord.**

Expect to leave your *PAST* in your PAST

Past: The history of a person, country, or institution; A part of a person's history that is (considered to be) shameful.

1. **Isaiah 43:18-19 (NLT) But forget all that-it is nothing compared to what I am going to do. For I am about to do something new. See, I have already begun! Do you not see it? I will make a pathway through the wilderness...**

2. Psalm 25:7 (NASB) Do not remember the sins of my youth or my wrongdoings; Remember me according to Your faithfulness, For Your goodness' sake, LORD.

3. **1st John 1:9 (KJV) If we confess our sins, he is faithful and just to forgive us our sins, and to cleanse us from all unrighteousness.**

4. Luke 9:62 (KJV) And Jesus said unto him, no man, having put his hand to the plough, and looking back, is fit for the kingdom of God.

5. **Philippians 3:13-14 (NLT) No, dear brothers and sisters, I have not achieved it, but I focus on this one thing: Forgetting the PAST and looking forward to what lies ahead, I press on to reach the end of the race and receive the heavenly prize for which God, through Christ Jesus, is calling us.**

6. 2nd Corinthians 5:17 (KJV) Therefore, if any man be in Christ, he is a new creature: old things are PASSED away; behold, all things are become new.

7. **Psalm 103:12-13 (NLT) He has removed our sins as far from us as the east is from the west. The Lord is like a father to his children, tender and compassionate to those who fear him.**

8. Genesis 41:51 (ESV) Joseph called the name of the firstborn Manasseh. "For", he said, "God has made me FORGET all my hardship and all my father's house."

9. **Isaiah 43:25 (NCV) I, I am the One who erases all your sins for my sake; I will not remember your sins.**

10. Proverbs 4:25 (NLT) Look straight ahead, and fix your eyes on what lies before you.

11. **Lamentations 3:22-23 (HCSB) Because of the Lord's faithful love we do not perish, for His mercies never end. They are NEW every morning; great is Your faithfulness!**

Expect to take *COMMUNION*

Communion: an act or instance of sharing. A Christian sacrament in which consecrated bread and wine are consumed as memorials of Christ's death or as symbols for the realization of a spiritual union between Christ and communicant or as the body and blood of Christ.

1. **Matthew 26:26-28 (NIV) While they were eating, Jesus took bread, and when he had given thanks, he broke it and gave it to his disciples, saying, "Take and eat; this is my body." Then he took a cup, and when he had given thanks, he gave it to them, saying, "Drink from it, all of you. This is my blood of the covenant, which is poured out for many for the forgiveness of sins."**

2. 1st Corinthians 11:26 (NLT) For every time you eat this bread and drink this cup, you are announcing the Lord's death until he comes again.

3. **John 6:53-58 (NIV) Jesus said to them, "Very truly I tell you, unless you eat the flesh of the Son of Man and drink his blood, you have no life in you. Whoever eats my flesh and drinks my blood has eternal life, and I will raise them up at the last day. For my flesh is real food and my blood is real drink. Whoever eats my flesh and drinks my blood remains in me, and I in them. Just as the living Father sent me and I live because of the Father, so the one who feeds on me will live because of me. This is the bread that came down from heaven. Your ancestors ate manna and died, but whoever feeds on this bread will live forever."**

4. Luke 22:19 (NIV) And he took bread, gave thanks and broke it, and gave it to them, saying, "This is my body given for you; do this in remembrance of me."

Expect to *GIVE* as unto the Lord

Give: To cause or allow (someone or something) to have something; donate; to provide or supply with.

1. **Luke 3:11 (NIV) John answered, "Anyone who has two shirts should share with the one who has none, and anyone who has food should do the same."**

2. Acts 20:35 (NLT) And I have been a constant example of how you can help those in need by working hard. You should remember the words of the Lord Jesus: "It is more blessed to give than to receive."

3. **Psalm 37:21 (NLT) The wicked borrow and never repay, but the godly are generous givers.**

4. Proverbs 3:27 (NLT) Do all you can for everyone who deserves your help.

5. **2nd Corinthians 9:7 (NCV) Each of you should give as you have decided in your heart to give. You should not be sad when you give, and you should not give because you feel forced to give. God loves the person who gives happily.**

6. Malachi 3:10 (Amplified) "Bring all the tithes (the tenth) into the storehouse, so that there may be food in My house, and test Me now in this," says the LORD of hosts, "if I will not open for you the windows of heaven and pour out for you (so great) a blessing until there is no more room to receive it."

7. **Proverbs 18:16 (NLT) Giving a gift can open doors; it gives access to import people!**

8. Proverbs 3:9 (NLT) Honor the LORD with your wealth and with the best part of everything you produce.

9. **Proverbs 11:25 (NKJV) The generous soul will be made rich. And he who waters will also be watered himself.**

10. Luke 6:38 (NLT) Give, and you will receive...

Expect to *FAST* sacrificially as unto the Lord

Fast: abstain from all or some kinds of food or drink, especially as a religious observance.

1. **Joel 2:12 (NCV) The Lord says, "Even now, come back to me with all your heart. FAST, cry, and be sad."**

2. Luke 2:37 (GW) and she had been a widow for 84 years. Anna never left the temple courtyard but worshipped day and night by FASTING and praying.

3. **Matthew 6:17-18 (NCV) So when you FAST, comb your hair and wash your face. Then people will not know that you are FASTING, but your Father, whom you cannot see, will see you. Your Father sees what is done in secret, and he will reward you.**

4. Acts 14:23 (NCV) They chose elders for each church, by praying and FASTING for a certain time…

5. **Daniel 10:3 (NKJV) I ate no pleasant food, no meat or wine came into my mouth, nor did I anoint myself at all, till three whole weeks were fulfilled.**

6. Esther 4-16 (NIV) "Go, gather together all the Jews who are in Susa, and FAST for me. Do not eat or drink for three days, night or day…"

7. **Luke 5:35 (CSB) But the time will come when the groom will be taken away from them-then they will FAST in those days.**

Expect to have *FELLOWSHIP* with God and Man

Fellowship: a group of people meeting to pursue a shared interest or aim.

1. **1ˢᵗ Corinthians 1:9 (ESV) God is faithful, by whom you were called into the FELLOWSHIP of his Son, Jesus Christ our Lord.**

2. 2ⁿᵈ Corinthians 13:14 (ESV) The grace of the Lord Jesus Christ and the love of God and the FELLOWSHIP of the Holy Spirit be with you all.

3. **Hebrews 10:24-25 (ESV) And let us consider how to stir up one another to love and good works, not neglecting to meet together, as is the habit of some, but encouraging one another, and all the more as you see the Day drawing near.**

4. Proverbs 27:17 (ESV) Iron sharpens iron, and one man sharpens another.

5. **Acts 2:42 (GW) The disciples were devoted to the teachings of the apostles, to FELLOWSHIP, to the breaking of bread, and to prayer.**

6. Ecclesiastes 4:9-12 (NLT) Two people are better off than one, for they can help each other succeed. If one person falls, the other can reach out and help. But someone who falls alone is in real trouble. Likewise, two people lying close together can keep each other warm. But how can one be warm alone? A person standing alone can be attacked and defeated, but two can stand back-to-back and conquer. Three are even better, for a triple-braided cord is not easily broken.

7. **Matthew 18:20 (ESV) For where two or three are gathered in my name, there am I among them.**

email <u>smithbuffie@gmail.com</u> for questions and speaking engagements...

Printed in the United States
by Baker & Taylor Publisher Services